Memory

David Moxon

Memory

David Moxon

To Karen, Hannah and Naomi

Heinemann Educational Publishers
Halley Court, Jordan Hill, Oxford, OX2 8EJ
a division of Reed Educational & Professional Publishing Ltd

OXFORD MELBOURNE AUCKLAND
JOHANNESBURG BLANTYRE GABORONE
IBADAN PORTSMOUTH NH(USA) CHICAGO

Text © David Moxon, 2000
First published in 2000

04 03 02 01 00
9 8 7 6 5 4 3 2 1

British Library Cataloguing in Publication Data
A catalogue record for this book is available from the British Library

ISBN 0 435 806521

Typeset by Wyvern 21 Ltd
Picture research by Liz Eddison
Illustration by Paul Beebee at Beehive Illustration
Printed and bound in Great Britain by The Bath Press Ltd., Bath

Acknowledgements
The authors and publishers would like to thank the following for the use of copyright material:
Cambridge University Press for the extract from *Remembering*, Bartlett, F. C. (1932) on p. 24; for the extract from 'A method for increasing patients recall of information presented by doctors', Ley, P., Bradshaw, P. W., Eaves, D. and Walker, C. M. *Psychological Medicine*, vol. 3 on p. 50; Department of Health for the material on pp. 46, 47. © Crown Copyright 1999; Express Newspapers for the extract from 'After everything else, now GM scientists take the kick out of a cup of coffee', Ben Dipietro, *Daily Express*, 17/9/99 on p. 30; Health Development Agency for the material on p. 46. © Crown Copyright 1999; Lombard Direct for the material on p. 44.

The publishers would like to thank the following for permission to use photographs: Professor Robert Buckout/Robert Wm Shomer Ph.D., p. 22; Science Photo Library/Petit Format, p. 2; Walkers Crisps, p. 44.

Cover photograph by AKG London

The publishers have made every effort to trace the copyright holders, but if they have inadvertently overlooked any, they will be pleased to make the necessary arrangements at the first opportunity.

Tel: 01865 888058 www.heinemann.co.uk

Y0055026

C) Contents

Chapter 4

1 Introduction

Memory is an area of psychology that has a long past. A lot of research has been published within this field, and many theories and explanations have been put forward as to why we remember and forget.

As with any topic within psychology, theories only become useful when they are applied to real life. One of the features of this book and indeed this whole series is its emphasis on real life applications. In this book we consider how memory affects all aspects of our lives, from medicine through to marketing.

This book is divided into four chapters, with each chapter considering an aspect of memory.

Chapter 1

This chapter is concerned with defining and explaining memory, and also tracing its history by looking at key researchers. It ends by setting out some of the ground work for Chapter 2 by outlining key ideas and concepts within memory research.

Chapter 2

This chapter is devoted to models and theories of memory. It gives detailed accounts of the explanations and highlights issues that arise from these explanations.

Chapter 3

This chapter is devoted to forgetting. It considers theories of why we forget and applies these to real life phenomenon.

Chapter 4

Finally, in this chapter we tie all the previous ideas together by considering real life applications of memory. At the end of this chapter there is a 'theory cross-reference section', which links together the real life applications and theories from previous chapters. It acts as a useful resource for you to apply your knowledge.

How to use this book

This book has a number of features to help you understand the topic more easily. It is written to give you a wide range of skills in preparation for any of the new AS and A level psychology syllabi. Below is a list of the features with a brief summary to explain how to use them.

1 Real Life Applications

These consist of 'text boxes' which develop further a concept already discussed within the main text. Often they provide articles or outlines of studies. In all cases they attempt to apply theory to real life situations.

2 Commentary

These paragraphs appear throughout the book. They follow on from issues raised within the main text. They serve a number of functions: to provide an evaluation of the earlier text, to clarify a point or to highlight some related issue. Sometimes they provide 'for' and 'against' debates.

3 Key studies

As the title implies these are descriptions of important studies within a specific area. There are two of these for each chapter. They briefly identify the aims, method, results and conclusions of the study. This feature helps you to understand the methodology of research.

4 Questions

Each 'Real Life Application' has two or three short answer questions, designed to test a range of skills including: summarising, outlining and evaluating. All of these activities are designed to allow you to acquire the study skills outlined within the syllabi.

In addition, two or three 'essay style' questions are included at the end of each chapter. They relate specifically to the material covered within that chapter.

5 Advice on answering questions

At the end of the book there is a short section that gives brief advice on answering all the essay and short answer questions presented in this book.

1 What is memory and what is it for?

This chapter considers three areas: how we can define memory, a brief history of memory research and concepts within memory research. It focuses on evolutionary explanations, seven influential figures in the development of the study of memory, general concepts related to memory and issues including metamemory, photographic memory, and episodic and procedural memories. Real Life Applications that are considered are:

- RLA 1: Memories of the womb
- RLA 2: Ancient memories within therapy
- RLA 3: Childhood memories
- RLA 4: Memory and Artificial Intelligence
- RLA 5: Mnemonics – improving encoding to improve retrieval
- RLA 6: Metamemory
- RLA 7: Photographic memory.

Memory is the name given to the ability we have to remember things from the past. The past might include a few seconds ago, a few hours ago, a few months ago or many years ago. In fact, some scientists believe that it is possible to remember our birth and womb experiences.

Real Life Application 1:

Memories of the womb

A fascinating study was reported in *Science*, back in 1984. It was an experiment carried out by De Casper and Fifer, and it demonstrated that unborn babies could remember sounds they had heard in the womb. The investigators asked sixteen pregnant women to read aloud *The cat in the hat*, a famous children's book by Dr Seuss, twice a day for the last six and a half weeks of pregnancy. When the babies were born, and they were old enough to control their sucking reflex, they were tested in a preference study.

Because you can't ask a newborn which it prefers, a clever technique was employed to test the baby's preferences. It was given a dummy, which was connected to tape recordings of the mother's voice, in one condition reading *The cat in the hat* (the story it had been exposed to in the womb) and in the other condition the mother reading a similar but different story (one that it had not been exposed to in the womb). The babies showed a significant preference for *The cat in the hat*.

Because the mother had been reading both stories, it can be assumed that it couldn't have been a preference for the mother's voice, it must have been the story. This research suggests that unborn babies are able to remember womb (uterine) experiences and show a preference for these experiences because they are familiar, therefore comforting.

Article adapted from *Science*, 1984, pp. 225, 302–303.

Summary

- There is evidence that once the human nervous system reaches a certain level of maturity, learning can take place within the womb (in utero).
- De Casper and Fifer (1984) used a preference technique to show that newborn babies prefer a

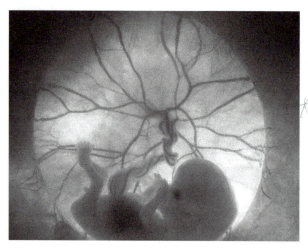

story they were read 'in utero' to another story of a similar type.

- The study referred to in this article suggests that some kind of memory took place prenatally. The precise nature of what a foetus can hear and then remember remains a mystery.

Questions

1 Outline some implications of babies being able to remember 'in utero'.

2 Identify an advantage and a disadvantage of De Casper and Fifer's method.

Defining memory

Investigators throughout history have attempted to express in simple terms what memory is. Famous quotations regarding the nature of memory include the following:

- *'To remember is to live'* (Martin Buber).

- *'If we remembered everything we should be as ill as if we remembered nothing'* (William James).

- *'Man differs in memory from brutes, and this is because there is record only of man'* (medical manuscript of AD 1380).

Albert Einstein was once asked about the minimum knowledge every student should possess. He replied: 'I don't really know. Personally, I never clutter up my memory with facts I can easily find in an encyclopaedia.'

Definitions of memory include the following:

- *'Memory is the mental function of retaining information about stimuli, events, images, ideas and so on after the original stimuli are no longer present'* (Penguin dictionary of psychology).

- *'Memory is the ability to keep things in one's mind or recall them at will'* (The Oxford dictionary).

Definitions are useful. However, they can never fully explain the complexities of remembering. Reber (1985) proposes that within the psychological literature, definitions of memory are numerous and have varied meanings. He goes on to suggest that as a result of this, memory is used almost invariably with some adjective proceeding it. This helps to set the limits on the kind of memory processes under discussion. Examples of this include *semantic* memory, *episodic* memory, *long term/short term* memory, *flashbulb* memory and so on. All of these concepts will be looked at in more detail later in this book.

What is the purpose of memory?

Why do we have this ability and what is its purpose? Some scientists regard survival as the primary imperative of memory. In an evolutionary sense, if our ancestors were able to recall potential dangers, they could learn avoidance strategies. Also, memories that could be passed on from generation to generation would be useful; this would allow many behaviours to be 'instinctual'.

Biological memory: our survival memory

Within scientific literature there is a concept referred to as 'biological memory' or 'genetic memory'. It is argued that the human species (*Homo sapiens*) has the ability to pass on important survival information in the genes. The genetic code predisposes us to behave in certain ways. Therefore, the survival information is not within our conscious awareness. For example, you may not know why you're scared of the dark or heights, but clearly avoiding these things 'ups' your chances of survival.

Tinbergen (1951) proposed that every animal species possesses a repertoire of behaviours, and that they are activated by certain stimuli within the environment. He referred to these as innate releasing mechanisms (IRM). The mallard duck engages in courtship behaviour at the sight of the green crested head of the male mallard. Goslings follow their mothers immediately after hatching. But who taught these animals to behave this way? They were not taught – it is instinctual. They are biologically predisposed to engage in these behaviours. Clearly, the 'memory' within the genes is making sure that they survive. In fact, Gardner (1988) coined the term 'master programmes', which illustrates the importance he placed on these genetic memories.

It makes evolutionary sense to pass behavioural predispositions on from one generation to the next, but is it possible that emotional memories can be passed on in the same way?

Real Life Application 2:
Ancient memories within therapy

Material A: Jung's archetypes

Jung (1875–1961) attached relatively little importance to our individual past. Unlike Freud, he saw the personal unconscious having marginal effect on our later behaviour. Rather than our own unconscious, personal childhood memories shaping who we are, Jung believed it was our collective unconscious. This is an unconscious 'cooking pot' that contains emotions and feelings which had all been experienced by our ancestors from previous generations. In fact, Jung believed we could trace the collective unconscious back to the dawn of humankind.

The collective unconscious is a reservoir of images called primordial images which relate to the first or original development of the psyche, human, pre-human and animal. (Hall and Norby, 1973)

Clearly the implication of this type of unconscious is that our behaviour is affected by 'memories' of emotions experienced by our ancestors. Perhaps this shouldn't be too surprising when you think that our eye and hair colour are influenced by those same people. Jung referred to these earliest symbolic memories as archetypes.

Material B: Activating ancient memories in dramatherapy

Dramatherapy is the intentional (planned) use of the healing aspects of drama in the therapeutic process (British Association of Dramatherapy, 1991).

In simple terms through mediums such as enactment, music making, painting and sculpting, clients are encouraged to allow feelings and emotions to surface, within the safety of the therapeutic environment.

In a Freudian sense, many of these experiences will be recovered from our childhood. However,

as you have just read in Material A it could be suggested that the emotions we recall during dramatherapy could stem from our collective unconscious. Not only do we have a personal unconscious history, we also share an unconscious with our ancestors.

Often in dramatherapy, clients find inspiration or 'inner abilities', which can be totally unexpected.

Sometimes when making music, clients can get so 'carried away' with beating drums, that they appear to be connecting with memories of behaviours that their ancient ancestors engaged in.
(Annie Wilson, 1999 dramatherapy tutor).

Summary

- Jung developed the idea of the collective unconscious. He proposed that it consisted of the feelings and emotions of our ancestors – a sort of evolutionary memory.
- Jung believed that the collective unconscious contains primitive symbols – ideas that have unconscious meanings to us. He referred to these as archetypes.
- Some researchers believe that it is possible to see 'archetypal' behaviour manifest itself within therapy. Because dramatherapy uses a variety of creative mediums, it is a very good example of this.
- It must be remembered that both 'biological memory' and the 'collective unconscious' are hypothetical ideas. Scientists have not discovered the unconscious gene. It is not feasible that memories could be passed from generation to generation by any other means. So at present, the concept of 'ancient memories' is just an interesting idea.

Questions

1 Outline a major problem in verifying Jung's proposals.

2 Identify some ways in which the recalling of 'primitive memories' could be useful within therapy, and some ways in which they could be dangerous.

More recently, there is evidence that modern scientists are beginning to 'embrace' the idea of a collective unconscious. In his book *Awareness: What it is, what it does* (1996), psychiatrist Chris Nunn ponders the implications of archetypes. He suggests that:

Maybe people can get access to stray memories imprinted on the fabric of the universe that are not part of their own personal histories.

This could be an alternative explanation of past life experiences. Clearly, a lot more work is needed in this area. However, it is quite fascinating to think that we all may have a reservoir of memories, potentially hundreds of thousands of years old.

A brief history of memory research

In this part of the chapter, we will take a look at seven influential figures in the development of the study of memory. Their contribution will be outlined and the implications of their ideas assessed.

It is obvious that we are not the first people to ask questions about the nature of memory. As we have already seen earlier in this chapter, it could be assumed that our cave-dwelling ancestors must have wondered why they had this ability to remember things, from one day to the next. Philosophers throughout history have also pondered the nature of memory.

The ancient Greeks

The ancient Greeks developed a method of memory improvement that became known as mnemonics after the Greek goddess of memory (see RLA 5, Material A on pages 12–13).

Aristotle published an essay entitled 'Memory', in which he attempted to describe the features of recall. It is proposed by many that this is the first formal attempt at understanding this subject.

Plato likened memory to a wax tablet: 'We hold the wax to perceptions and thoughts, and in that receive the impression of them.' Ironically, this idea that a 'mental impression' is created inside the mind is strangely similar to modern explanations of memory – the difference being that current views of memory emphasize its dynamic nature, rather than seeing it as a static 'storage bin' that collects experiences.

Commentary

- The ideas put forward by the ancient Greeks lacked scientific rigour. However, the Greeks did begin the process of formally recording investigations into memory.
- Some contemporary academics (for example Kline, 1988), would argue that insights into any discipline should not be devalued just because they do not use the Western 'scientific method'.

William James

In 1890, William James published what is regarded by many as the first textbook of psychology. His comprehensive coverage of the subject contained many topics, including memory.

James believed that memory served a vital function, allowing us to retain certain bits of information invaluable for our survival. His idea was that we do not need to remember every piece of sensory information we are exposed to, as this would overload us with trivial data. He went on to suggest that we have two memory systems: 'primary memory', a system that allows us to experience consciousness; and 'secondary memory', a system that allows us to store events from the past.

Access to the primary memory required very little effort, whereas secondary memory required a deliberate effortful act. As we will see later, this idea has been taken much further by contemporary research.

Commentary

- James provided us with a solid foundation within the field of memory. His notions of a primary and secondary memory system set the scene for what later became interpreted as short term memory and long term memory (STM and LTM).
- James's ideas about memory did not really start to influence experimental psychology until the 1960s – the reason being that up until this time, behaviourism was the dominant force within psychology. James's focus on consciousness and memory did not fit into the objective approach of the behaviourists, so his earlier theories tended to be ignored (Parkin, 1993).

Hermann Ebbinghaus

Hermann Ebbinghaus (1850-1909), who originally trained in philosophy, suggested that:

Mental states of every kind – sensations, feelings, ideas – which were at one time present in consciousness (but have now disappeared from it), have not with their disappearance absolutely ceased to exist.

In his book *Memory: A contribution to experimental psychology* (1885), he goes on further:

... they continue to exist, stored up so to speak, in the memory.

So for Ebbinghaus, experiences never cease to exist, they just get 'stored up' in memory. He continues to explain in his book that there are three ways in which the memory store may be accessed. First, he describes voluntary access, in which we deliberately try to recollect images. Second, he outlines a recall that is 'without any act of the will – images that are reproduced involuntarily'. Third, he proposes that there is a type of recall that is obvious only because we are able to carry out some task or activity. It is knowledge that is not conscious, yet produces effects that can be seen in everyday life. As we will see in Chapter 2, modern researchers have developed similar ideas to Ebbinghaus, but have used different terms.

One very important contribution that Ebbinghaus made to the development of memory research was the rigour in his methodology. The experiments he conducted tested how humans learned to associate words together. He was more interested in the process of memory formation than the end result. For this reason he developed 'nonsense syllables', combinations of letters that had no existing associations.

His argument was that if he used words that already existed some of those words would be easier to recall than others because they would be well established in the memory storage. For example, if a person was to see the word 'cage' and they owned a pet that was kept in a cage, they would be at a distinct advantage when it came to remembering this word. They could make a more meaningful association than someone who did not own such a pet.

This sounds like a very sensible approach to memory research – to use material that has no preconceived images attached to it. However, in 1928 a psychologist named Glaze suggested that perhaps Ebbinghaus's 'nonsense syllables' weren't such nonsense after all. Given the opportunity most people could infer some association to the syllables. For example, I could present you with the following three-letter nonsense syllables:

TVR   RTA   TBA

The first is an abbreviation of Trevor, the first name of the engineer who developed the TVR sports car (based at Blackpool, Great Britain). The second is a common medical abbreviation for a 'road traffic accident' and the third is a commonly used abbreviation in English for 'to be arranged'. So as can be seen, we can make sense of what appears to be impossible three-letter words.

Because of the meticulous control Ebbinghaus used in his experiments he concluded that anything we learn is forgotten more quickly in the first few hours than it is later on. Also by using 'nonsense syllables' he demonstrated that words with no apparent meaning to us are much more difficult to remember than those with existing associations. These two contributions are still recognized today.

However, there are two serious drawbacks to Ebbinghaus's work. First, he conducted the experiments on himself. Over a period of about five years he worked alone, with no real supervision. Even though one must admire his experimental preciseness, the fact remains that his results were obtained through the case study method. Ebbinghaus identified some interesting features of his own memory, but great caution must be exercised when attempting to generalize the results to the population as a whole. Second, because Ebbinghaus used nonsense syllables, it could be argued that his experiments do not reflect memory in the real world (that is, they lack ecological validity).

Commentary

- Ebbinghaus was the first to use a systematic and scientific approach to the investigation of memory.
- However, researchers such as Bartlett (1932; see page 6) suggested that Ebbinghaus's approach had very little to do with memory in our everyday life. It was too artificial because it was based in the laboratory.
- The clever idea that Ebbinghaus had to create non-meaningful syllables, so as to prevent any preconceived ideas, ironically can also be seen as a shortcoming. 'Nonsense syllables' are representative of real life.
- Because Ebbinghaus used himself as the participant, great caution should be exercised when generalising his findings to the wider population.

KEY STUDY 1

Researcher: Ebbinghaus (1885)

Aims: The aim of this study was to explain how memory works, in particular how we learn 'nonsense material'.

Method: Ebbinghaus created 2,300 'nonsense syllables' and attempted to learn sequences of them, selected at random. He repeated a series until he could repeat them without error. The reading and recitation took place at a constant rate of 150 strokes per minute (a metronome was used). Also, he always tested himself between the hours of 1 p.m. and 3 p.m.

Results: When Ebbinghaus could correctly recall two consecutive repetitions of a series he proposed it had been learnt. Often he would return to a series in an attempt to learn it again. He recorded how many times it took him to relearn the series. He proposed that time was related to memory loss. (He used the term 'obliviscence' – an old-fashioned term for loss of information from memory.) He concluded that shorter series of nonsense syllables are forgotten (over time) more quickly than longer ones. He also found that varying the length of delay in recall had significant effects on memorability. Delays of 10 or 20 minutes showed very sharp decline in recall, whereas delays of hours or indeed days, showed a significant levelling off (see Figure 1.1 below).

Conclusions: Memory is affected by repetition and delays in recall.

Frederic Bartlett

In 1932, Frederick Bartlett (1886–1969) published a pioneering text entitled *Remembering*. It was groundbreaking because, unlike any of the afore-mentioned historical figures, he suggested that recall is not just the reactivation of events from some sort of 'storage bin', but a whole new re-processing in its own right. He argued that we use existing 'structures of knowledge' (a concept he called 'schemas') to help in the 'reforming' of the original memories. Therefore our attitudes, expectations, beliefs and levels of motivation will highly influence the way in which we remember.

Commentary

- Bartlett's ideas regarding memory have had far-reaching implications. As we will see in Chapter 4, his theories really 'come into their own' when we start to apply them to real life situations.
- Because Bartlett focused on the interaction between memory function and other cognitive processes, it can be seen as quite a complex approach, particu-

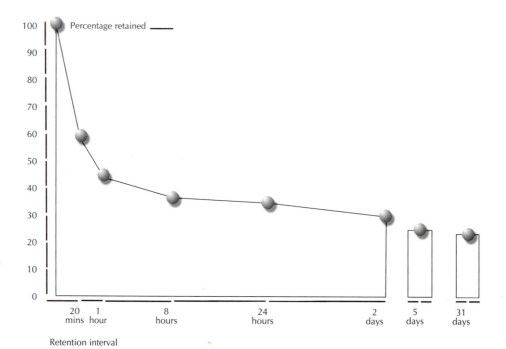

This is the dramatic curve that Ebbinghaus obtained when he plotted the results of one of his forgetting experiments on himself. His finding, that information loss is very rapid at first and then levels off, holds good for many types of learned material.

Figure 1.1: Retention intervals

larly when compared to the more simplistic Ebbinghaus theories (Baddeley, 1976).

Sigmund Freud

Sigmund Freud (1856–1939) was the controversial founder of psychoanalysis. His major contribution to the field of memory research was an explanation of why we forget. He developed the concept of 'motivated forgetting'. Memories that we find too painful or traumatic are 'banished' from our unconscious awareness and therefore appear to be forgotten. However, under certain circumstances they can resurface – often causing us discomfort and emotional distress.

Freud suggested that the early years of our life are forgotten (a concept he referred to as 'infantile amnesia'). But in exactly the same way as motivated forgetting, the emotional experiences of these formative years are 'locked away' within the unconscious, and resurfacing can lead to neurosis.

Commentary

- This is very much a separate explanation of why we forget and doesn't really tie in with any other major theoretical perspective. In some ways this gives it a unique appeal.
- It is very difficult to assess the validity of Freud's ideas. To set up a laboratory experiment that created psychological trauma in participants would be unethical.
- However, some studies have managed to create unpleasant events for participants within a controlled environment. Researchers such as Kline (1972) and Erdelyi (1985) suggest that on a number of occasions 'motivated forgetting appears to be present'.
- This concept has been applied widely in areas of research such as public health scares where high levels of anxiety affect memorability of information.

Real Life Application 3

Childhood memories

Material A: What happens to our childhood memories?

According to researchers such as Usher and Neisser, who published the findings of an experiment in the *Journal of experimental psychology* in 1993, the average person can accurately recall a few autobiographical ('story-type') memories from age five or six, but remember virtually nothing before the age of three. Why is this so?

Different theories have been proposed to explain this 'childhood amnesia'. Some researchers such as Bauer (1996), published in the *American psychologist*, suggests that the reason young children forget the early years is because their 'cognitive frameworks' (memory hardware) are insufficiently mature to store the events. This leads us into another problem however: does this lack of maturity mean that events are not stored at all, or is it the case that they are stored but in later life we cannot readily access them?

Sigmund Freud explained childhood amnesia in terms of motivated forgetting. He argued that events and experiences that were too painful to be kept in our conscious minds were 'banished' to the unconscious. What is curious about this explanation is that it would imply that virtually all of our earliest memories must have been traumatic.

Material B: False memory syndrome

As we already discussed in Material A, there are a number of complex issues which, as yet, have to be resolved regarding childhood amnesia. A recent issue, which renewed interest in this area, began to emerge in the early 1990s. Patients undergoing psychotherapy – particularly psychoanalysis – began reporting early childhood memories of sexual abuse.

Ten years ago Lydia Carney led the enviable, untroubled life of the quintessential middle-class wife. What started off as depression resulting from the death of a close friend soon turned into severe chronic depression which required psychotherapy. During the sessions, her analyst suggested that she had been sexually abused by her father. Today Lydia thinks the allegations are nonsense. However, because her father died in 1993, she feels terrible guilt that she was not speaking to him prior to his death.

Extract adapted from *The Sunday Times*, 29 March 1998.

The question that arises from newspaper articles such as this one is: 'How reliable is "repressed memory testimony"?' One major problem in assessing the validity of memories from the first four years of life is that they may not be retrievable in an adult form (that is, using words). The early memories may have been encoded in an 'emotional form', which could well manifest itself in terms of behaviour and negative feelings.

According to a British Psychological Society report on false memory syndrome published in

1995, for the reason mentioned above some child-hood recall could be false. But what of the accusers themselves? In the March 1997 edition of *The Psychologist*, Gudjonsson surveyed members of the British False Memory Society (BFMS – a self-help group for accused families, set up in 1993). He found that more accusers were predominantly female, middle class and had above-average school or educational achievement. The author does, however, acknowledge that the less educated, manual workers and minority groups are less likely to know about and join groups such as the BFMS. This could go some way to explain these findings.

Summary

- None of us has a very accurate recall of the first five or six years of our life.
- The two major explanations for this fact are provided by researchers such as Bauer and Freud.
- People undergoing psychotherapy are particularly vulnerable to having their early memories distorted, which has led to the phenomena known as 'false memory syndrome'.
- In 1993 the British False Memory Society (BFMS) was set up to help and support those families accused of abuse.

Questions

1 In your own words, outline the different explanations given for childhood amnesia.

2 What is false memory syndrome?

Donald Hebb

Donald Hebb (1904–1985), studied memory from a physiological perspective. In 1949 he published a book entitled *The organization of behaviour* in which he suggested that as we learn, connections are 'reinforced' between nerve cells. Prior to this reinforcement, nerve cells reverberate with the processing of new information. Hebb saw this reverberation as STM. He argued that after about 30 seconds of activity, permanent pathways form. These pathways create complex groupings of nerve cells, which he referred to as 'cell assemblies'. It is the creation of these permanent cell groupings that Hebb saw as the biological basis of LTM.

Commentary

- Hebb's theory was rooted in physiology and has influenced a whole perspective in the study of memory – namely the biological point of view.
- He suggested that there was a physiological distinction between STM and LTM.
- Evidence to back up the STM-LTM dichotomy comes from laboratory studies (for example Duncan, 1949) and from clinical studies of amnesic patients.
- Hebb's ideas have been very influential in recent years, especially in the development of 'neural network models' within the field of Artificial Intelligence (see RLA 4 below). When applied to computing, chaos theory allows self-organising algorithms gradually to learn patterns of information (a similar idea to Hebb's cell assemblies). By being able to remember their own experiences and learn from them, some suggest that the intelligence of machines will soon exceed that of humans (Kurzweil, 1999).

Real Life Application 4:

Memory and Artificial Intelligence

In the early 1980s scientists working within the field of Artificial Intelligence (AI), began developing ideas in an attempt to make computers 'think' more like humans. One of the most influential of these ideas became known as the parallel distributed processing (PDP) model. The reasoning behind this was that human minds are able to carry out cognitive processing simultaneously in many parts of the brain. If computers were to mimic humans, they would need to be able to do this also.

One interesting feature about memory is that it doesn't take place within a specified area of the brain. It is represented by 'groups' of nerve cells distributed throughout the brain. When we recall existing memories, different connections are reactivated within the groups and the original idea is regenerated. This would mean that if a computer wanted to recall information like a human, it would have to involve complex networks or groups of information in the recall process. If new data had suggested that a modification was necessary, then the computer would strengthen the memory of the new information and weaken the old accordingly. The computer would be learning through experience.

Summary

- The parallel distribution processing model (PDP) was developed in an attempt to mimic the ability humans have to carry out cognitive processes simultaneously.
- Memory is represented within the human brain by 'groups of nerve cells' working in conjunction with one another. The PDP model attempts to copy this.
- By including memory within this model, scientists are able to programme machines to remember their mistakes and alter their responses next time.

Questions

1 In your own words, describe the PDP model.

2 Why are 'network' models useful when attempting to make machines remember in the same way as humans?

Concepts within memory research

The second part of the chapter considers some general concepts related to memory. It starts by looking at the ways in which we 'take on board' information. Next it considers storage (both short term and long term). It then goes on to look at the ways in which information can be retrieved. This leads us to consider more general issues of memory including metamemory, photographic memory, and episodic and procedural memories.

As we have already seen there are many different ways of describing and defining memory. Throughout history, many researchers have contributed parts to the overall picture. This is inevitable, with a concept so complex as memory. Before we go on to

look at the major theories of why we can remember (in Chapter 2), we need to be introduced to some general concepts. As Figure 1.2 shows, there are three major processes involved in memory:

1 encoding,
2 storage and
3 retrieval.

We will look at each of these in turn in the text that follows.

Encoding

This is the name given to the process by which we 'take on board' information. Information can be obtained via any of the senses, but obviously we don't process and remember all the sensory information we receive as this would be a waste of energy.

The multistore model proposed by Atkinson and Shiffrin in 1968 (see Chapter 2), sees information entering memory via the sensory store. It argues that this is an extremely transient storage system, which retains information about the pattern of sensory stimulation (Parkin, 1993). The two most common sensory modes of storage are sight and sound. Iconic (image) memory is the term used to describe visual material; echoic memory describes sound.

Iconic memory

This term was developed by Sperling (1960). He found participants were able to recall with high levels of accuracy quite detailed information that was presented within time periods of less than half a second. It seems that people are able to 'hold' an image within memory, but this effect is very short lived.

Echoic memory

This is the auditory equivalent to iconic memory. Howell and Darwin (1977) conducted a study that illustrated this point. They found that phonemes (basic units of speech sounds) that were acoustically similar were recognized slightly quicker than those with acoustic differences. It seems that we are able to distinguish between sounds by retaining them in a sort of 'fleeting' memory system. This effect is very short lived (less than 800 milliseconds).

Commentary

Why do we have these abilities? As seen earlier in this chapter, perhaps it gives us an advantage in evolutionary terms. If perceptions of the environment can be

1.	ENCODING This is the 'taking on board' of information	SENSORY STORAGE (i) Iconic memory (ii) Echoic memory
2.	STORAGE This is the 'filing' of information	SHORT TERM MEMORY (i) Chunking LONG TERM MEMORY (i) Procedural memory (ii) Declarative memory
3.	RETRIEVAL	ACCESSIBILITY AVAILABILITY

Figure 1.2: Three processes of memory

'held' for fractions of a second, it could be just enough time to make informed decisions that might save our life.

Storage

This is a self-explanatory term that describes how memories are 'held'. Since the growth in popularity of personal computers, most people are familiar with the idea of data storage. As mentioned earlier in this chapter, William James (1890), was astute enough to conclude that we have two types of memory – an immediate memory and a more long lasting system. This distinction is now referred to as short term memory and long term memory (STM and LTM). The idea is that we process information in the short term, then pass it on to a more permanent long term storage.

Short term memory (STM)

Even before Hebb proposed the physiological basis for the STM and LTM dichotomy back in 1949, Ebbinghaus (1885) had suggested that memory which is not rehearsed ('repeated' – see Chapter 2 for more details) is limited in terms of how much it can retain. He suggested from his research that this amounted to about seven or eight items.

If you think about a telephone number, with the area code included, on average it comprises eleven digits (for example, a fictitious number in Oxford would be 01865 000111). This might explain why for many of us, when we are told a number (such as the one above), the only way to successfully remember it, without writing it down, is to keep repeating it to ourselves. This, of course, is an example of rehearsal (see the multi-store model in Chapter 2, page 16).

In fact, the multi-store model (Atkinson and Shiffrin, 1971) goes on to suggest that STM is also limited in time, a maximum of about 30 seconds. So STM is limited by how much information it can retain. How can we explain, then, why some people are able to recall larger amounts of information that as yet are only in STM?

Chunking

The answer to this question came in 1956, with the publication of a paper entitled 'The magical number seven, plus or minus two: some limits on our capacity for processing information' by George Miller.

Miller concurred with previous ideas that STM was limited on average to about seven 'bits' of information. However, what he went on to suggest was

that this could be increased if we grouped the 'bits' of information together into larger 'chunks'.

The example below explains how, previously, remembering a sequence of eleven numbers would be very difficult in STM.

'Bits' of information

1	2	3	4	5	6	7

Number to be remembered

2	0	0	0	1	0	6	6	9	9	9

However, chunking the numbers we could make it much easier, as can be seen below.

'Bits' of information

1	2	3	4	5	6	7

Number to be remembered

2000	1066	999

As you can now see we have remembered eleven numbers within three spaces, leaving four free to use for other 'bits' of information. If you are still wondering why the numbers have been grouped in this way, it is because they have meaning:

- 1 = the year 2000
- 2 = the year 1066 (the battle of Hastings), and
- 3 = 999 (the emergency telephone number).

Miller suggested that we use STM as a temporary store for information that we require on a day-to-day basis – for example, shopping lists or telephone numbers.

Commentary

STM is a concept that has been highly debated between researchers. As we will see in Chapter 2, theories such as the 'levels of processing model' (Atkinson and Shiffrin, 1968, 1971) used STM as a major feature, whereas theories such as the 'levels processing model' (Craik and Lockhart, 1972) do not explicitly use it.

Long term memory (LTM)

Unlike STM, LTM is seen to have almost unlimited capacity. And unlike personal computers, our brains do not require hardware upgrades to increase storage capacity. If information is rehearsed or encoded in a sufficiently meaningful way, it will be transferred to long term storage.

There are four major distinctions within LTM. These different types of memory appear to serve different functions and appear to work independently of one another. The first two are procedural memory and declarative memory. Tulving (1972) further divided declarative into semantic and episodic. Let us now look at each of these in turn.

Procedural memory

Researchers such as Anderson (1985) have looked at this concept of memories for carrying out procedures. Many of us can swim, but it would be very hard to remember and explain how we do it.

Ryle (1949) distinguishes between memories based on 'knowing that' and 'knowing how'. We know that we can or can't swim. And if we *can* swim, then we also remember *how to* swim. The complex movements and co-ordinations required to glide through the water are retained in the procedural long term store.

Commentary

There is some experimental evidence that appears to support procedural LTM. Chapter 4 considers the case of HM, a man who suffered from surgically induced amnesia. What was fascinating about his condition was that he would learn a task, then on subsequent occasions would show no recollection of having done it before. However, over time he became more skilled. We could argue that HM could remember how to do something, but not remember the task itself. This is a finding quite consistent with other amnesic patients (Parkin and Leng, 1993).

Declarative memory: semantic and episodic

The term 'declarative memory' was put forward by Squire (1980, 1987) as a way of grouping semantic and episodic memories. The best way to think of this is to consider the types of knowledge that you possess. Some of it is general knowledge; some is personal knowledge.

For example, I know what a desert looks like, even though I have never visited one. I know how to spell the word 'desert'. This is general knowledge about the world and is referred to as semantic memory. Tulving (1972) defines it as knowledge of language, rules and concepts.

Our personal knowledge, which is unique to us, is referred to as episodic memory. Tulving (1972) defines this as 'an individual's autobiographical record of past experience'. Knowing all about deserts ('semantic memory') is not the same memory as having personal experience of being in a desert ('episodic memory').

In 1985, Tulving modified his definition of semantic memory to 'memory that allows the individual to construct mental models of the world'. He went on to suggest that with semantic memory we don't need to know why we can remember something in order to carry out some task. He used the term **noetic** to describe this experience.

Commentary

Evidence that backs up this idea of noetic memory experiences, can often be found in the amnesia literature. Chapter 4 considers the case of HM, an amnesic patient who underwent a number of experiments to assess the extent of his memory impairment. In one of these, he was asked to draw objects by looking not directly at the page but through a mirror. This is clearly a difficult task for anyone. On repeating the task on subsequent occasions HM showed no recollection of doing it before. However, his speed and accuracy got better (Scoville and Milner, 1957). HM's semantic memory was fine, but his episodic memory was impaired.

Retrieval

So far we have looked at two of the major processes in memory – that is, encoding and storage. The third process is retrieval. As we will see in Chapter 3, a major explanation of why we forget is that memories are inaccessible.

Tulving and Pearlstone (1966) made the distinction between accessibility and availability. In other words, a piece of information may well be available in storage but the fact is we cannot access it.

How often have you seen someone in the street, perhaps said 'Hello' to them, but can't quite place where you know them from? This is a common experience. Mandler (1980) argues that we have to search our LTM until we can retrieve all the pieces of the jigsaw. We suddenly remember where we know them from.

A similar experience is referred to as the 'tip-of-the-tongue' phenomenon (Brown and McNeill, 1966). We are aware that we possess the correct information in storage. The problem is we can't quite access it at that moment.

Accessibility to stored information is governed by retrieval cues (Clifford, 1980). If we encode the information with a 'useful' retrieval cue, then we can use that to help us locate the information. In his classic book *Use your head*, Tony Buzan (1974) stresses the importance of organising the material you want to remember. In particular, he identifies mnemonics as a technique that allows 'retrieval cues' to be created. As he says: 'Memory is primarily an associative and linking process' (1982). By using existing knowledge and associating it with the things we want to remember, we are allowing the information to be located.

Commentary

Researchers can use a whole range of methods to allow participants to recall what they have learnt. Table 1.1 gives a selection with a summary of each highlighting some strengths and weaknesses.

Table 1.1: *Recalling what has been learnt*

Method	Strengths and weaknesses
Free recall	This is where the participants are given a blank sheet of paper and asked to recall as much as possible. This is the hardest type of retrieval as there are no cues to assist. Most examinations are like this.
Cued recall	This is where participants are given a certain amount of information – for example, a 'gapped handout' leaves blanks within text, but the text itself should be the clue. This is a useful technique, particularly if 'learners' are working on their own.
Identification	This is where participants are shown a list of items (some of which they have been presented with before) and asked to identify them. Multiple choice is a good example. This may appear to be the easiest method. However, if the other items are very similar to the correct one, people can often become confused.

Mnemonics

It was the ancient Greeks who developed a method of associating things they wanted to remember with representations already in their memories. This idea of 'linking' the two together became known as mnemonics, named after Mnenosyne, the Goddess of memory.

An example of a mnemonic – perhaps one you may remember from early childhood – associates a set of initials with the colours of the rainbow.

Richard	–	Red
Of	–	Orange
York	–	Yellow
Gave	–	Green
Battle	–	Blue
In	–	Indigo
Vain	–	Violet

Notice that the first letters of each word in the verse represent the first letters of each of the colours. As can be seen below (RLA 5, Material B), mnemonists use a variety of associations other than just first letters.

Real Life Application 5:
Mnemonics – improving encoding to improve retrieval

Material A: Mnemonists – record breakers

- Mamoon Tariq, from Pakistan, memorized a single pack of shuffled cards in 44.62 seconds, in Florida (USA) on the 14 June 1993.
- Dominic O'Brien, from Hertfordshire (England), memorized a single pack of shuffled cards in a time of 55.62 seconds, in Piccadilly (London) on the 29 May 1992.
- Bhanddanta Vicittabi Vumsa (1911-1993) recited 16,000 pages of Buddhist canonical texts in Rangoon in 1974.
- Gon Yangling, of China, has memorized more than 15,000 telephone numbers, according to the Xinhua News Agency.
- Hideaki Tomoyori, of Yokohama (Japan), recited the mathematical value 'pi' from memory to 40,000 places in 17 hours 21 minutes.

Factual information taken from the *Guinness Book of Records* (1994).

Material B: Mnemonists – what is their secret?

As already mentioned, mnemonics are a widely used technique. One method uses the first letters of each word of a verse to represent the first letter of each of the things you are trying to remember. Another method (to help remember numbers) uses the number of letters of the words of the verse to represent numerical values, as in the case of remembering pi. To remember pi to 20 decimal places, simply count the numbers of letters in each word (including the title of the rhyme). This should give 3.14159265358979323846.

Pie
I wish I could determine pi
Eureka cried the great inventor
Christmas pudding
Christmas pie
Is the problem's very centre.

Another major technique used by mnemonists is visualization or imagery. Tony Buzan, the author of *Use your head* and other memory-improving books, identifies a method that has been used since the seventeenth century. He refers to this as the 'number-shape link'. This involves replacing each number from 1 to 10 with a symbol. Again, as with the mnemonic methods, it is helpful if the symbols rhyme with the numbers. For example:

1	=	bun
2	=	shoe
3	=	tree
4	=	door ... and so on.

The idea then is to associate or link the items you wish to remember with the rhyming image. Tony Buzan gives the example of a person wishing to remember a table, a feather, a cat and a leaf. Using the technique, the person would:

1 imagine a bun on top of a fragile table
2 imagine his/her favourite shoe with a giant feather sticking out of it
3 imagine a tree with a cat stuck in the very top branches
4 imagine his/her bedroom door as a giant leaf.

Dominic O'Brien (whose name appears in RLA 5, Material A) suggests the more colourful and exaggerated the images are, the better they will stay in your mind. In fact, an American school that trains bar staff uses the colours of the ingredients in cocktails to help students remember complex drink orders.

Summary

- There are a variety of techniques that may be used to improve memory. Mnemonics use existing knowledge such as the use of a rhyme or acronym to 'attach' items to be learnt to.
- Throughout history, individuals have shown amazing abilities regarding memory. These include remembering the order of a pack of randomly shuffled cards in just over 44 seconds and remembering 'pi' to 40,000 places.
- Imagery is a technique that can be used to enhance memory recall. World record-holding mnemonists such as Dominic O'Brien suggest the more colourful and exaggerated we make images, the more likely we are to remember the items we are trying to recall.

Questions

1 In your own words, describe mnemonics.

2 How does this technique improve retrieval?

Metamemory

Stratton and Hayes (1999) define metamemory as: 'Knowledge about how one's memory works or what its limitations are.' Often, we are aware that there is something we need to remember, but we can't think what it is. It's almost as if there is a process within our memory that is constantly assessing our memory ability.

Are people good at being able to assess their ability to remember? Experimental evidence (for example Lachman *et al*, 1981 – see RLA 6) suggests that people are. Not only are people aware if they know something or not, but they are also aware of the extent to which they know something. Knowing appears to be on a gradient (Cohen *et al*, 1986).

Real Life Application 6:

Metamemory

Material A: Metamemory – how well can we judge our own memories?

An interesting study carried out by Lachman, Lachman and Thornesberry in 1981 investigated how well people could judge their own memories. Participants were given 190 general knowledge questions and asked not to guess the answers if they didn't know. They were then asked to rate those questions they previously didn't know the answers to in terms of 'feeling of knowing'. For example, they were asked 'Do you definitely not know?', 'Do you maybe not know?', 'Could you recognize the answer if told?' and 'Could you recall the correct answer if given more time or further hints?'.

After carrying out these ratings the participants were given a list of four answers – one of which was correct. They had to indicate whether their answer now was a wild guess, an educated guess, probably right or definitely right.

What was found was that people were very accurate at knowing whether they had picked the correct answer or not. Also, people tended to search longer for answers they thought they knew the answer to than those questions they knew they definitely did not know the answer to.

Adapted from *Developmental Psychology*, 15, pp. 543–51.

Material B: *Who wants to be a millionaire?* – an example of metamemory

The television channel ITV has run a highly successful programme for a number of series, entitled *Who wants to be a millionaire?* It's a quiz show in which contestants get the opportunity to win £1 million by correctly answering fifteen general knowledge questions. Contestants each start off with three 'lifelines', which give them the opportunity to find out the correct answer if they don't know or are unsure.

An interesting observation of this programme is that many of the contestants are very good at assessing their own memories. Each question has four 'answers' – one of which is correct.

Often contestants know the answer before the correct option appears. This is an example of being certain of their memory recall.

On other occasions, people are not totally sure of the answer and use a 'lifeline' to try to confirm it. This is an example of believing that the answer is in the memory store, but not being certain how accurately it will be retrieved.

Often, contestants are faced with questions that they know they do not have the answer to. There is no 'data' in the memory store. In these situations, many of them take the money they have accumulated up to that point, and leave.

Summary

- Lachman *et al* found that people were very accurate at assessing their own ability to recall something.
- They spent more time searching for answers that they knew were in 'memory storage' than ones they knew were not.
- The popular television show *Who wants to be a*

millionaire? exemplifies the concept of metamemory. Part of the skill required by contestants is to assess their own knowledge and decide whether they can remember a fact or not.

Questions

1 In your own words, describe metamemory.

2 What are the benefits of humans possessing 'metamemory ability'? (A hint: think about evolutionary explanations.)

KEY STUDY 2

Researchers: Lachman, Lachman and Thornesberry (1981)

Aims: The aim of this study was to see how accurately people can estimate how close they are to knowing an answer, if they do not know a particular piece of information.

Method: Participants were given 190 general knowledge questions to answer. They were asked not to guess the answers. They were instructed to either give an answer to the question or respond 'don't know'. Their response times were recorded. Participants were then asked to judge their level of 'not knowing' on all the questions they identified earlier as 'don't know'. The four choices were: 1 Definitely do not know; 2 Maybe do not know; 3 Could recognize answer if told; 4 Could recall answer if given hints and more time. After a short period of time participants were given a 'four multiple choice style answer' to those questions they had identified as 'don't know'. Also they were asked to use a 'scale of confidence' in their answers, where: 1 = wild guess; 2 = educated guess; 3 = probably right; 4 = Definitely right.

Results: Participants who identified the higher confidence ratings (3 and 4) were more likely to choose the correct answer. These participants were also more likely to choose 3 and 4 responses in 'level of not knowing'. Participants searched longer for items they thought they might know, even though their final response was incorrect.

Conclusions: People are good at judging whether or not they know something.

foreign language, she was able to recall it perfectly – even by starting at the bottom line and working backwards to the top. Not surprisingly, she was able to use her unusual memory skills to help her in exams at high school and college.

Article adapted from *Memory Observed* by Ulric Neisser, 1982.

Photographic (eidetic) memory

This is an interesting concept within memory research. It is based on the assumption that it's possible to store vast amounts of information by briefly 'scanning' the material. It's as though a 'mental photograph' has been taken and all the richness of detail has been preserved. Clearly it would be an amazing ability. But does it actually exist? The more scientific term for this is eidetic memory , which comes from the Greek 'eidos' meaning 'what is seen'.

About 5 per cent of school children within the population possess this ability to some degree, but almost no adults have it (Haber, 1979). Most psychologists would agree there is no such thing as a true' photographic memory. However, there are some intriguing case studies that seem to defy the theorists. The case of Elizabeth (see RLA 7) illustrates this point.

Commentary

Occasionally, there are cases that start off resembling eidetic memory, but fail to completely satisfy the criteria. Gummerman and Gray (1971) report the case of Nancy. Even though she had an amazing ability to replicate material, the researchers argued she had not met the stringent requirements for her to be classed as an 'eidetiker'.

Real Life Application 7:

Photographic memory

In Ulric Neisser's book *Memory observed*, he cites the case study reported by Charles Stromeyer (III), of Elizabeth the 'adult Eidetiker'. She has an amazing ability to 'fetch back' detailed images of pictures or text. Many years after reading a poem in a

Summary

- Photographic memory is a term given to describe an almost perfect replication of some observed material (usually observed for only a short period of time).
- It is more correctly referred to as 'eidetic memory'.
- About 5 per cent of children appear to have eidetic memory to some degree, but virtually no adults (Haber, 1979).

Questions

1 How does eidetic imagery relate to iconic memory?

2 Can you think of reasons why more children possess eidetic imagery than adults?

Example essay questions

1 Outline and evaluate the different approaches that have been proposed in the study of memory.

2 'The history of research into memory comprises individuals pursuing their own interests with little evidence of cohesion and progression.' Discuss.

3 a Outline *two* general concepts of memory.
b How useful are these concepts in understanding memory in everyday life?

This chapter considers six major theories, explaining how and why we remember. The theories build on the general concepts considered in Chapter 1. Theories looked at are the multi-store model, levels of processing approach, working memory model, schema theory, theories of imagery and organization and, finally, the biological models of memory. Real Life Applications that are considered are:

- RLA 8: Schema theory and criminal faces
- RLA 9: Organization in memory
- RLA 10: 'Smart drugs' – drugs that enhance memory
- RLA 11: The physiology of memory
- RLA 12: Physical health and memory deterioration.

The first major theory to integrate a sensory storage, short term memory (STM) and long term memory (LTM) was the multi-store model developed by Atkinson and Shiffrin (1968, 1971; see Figure 2.1 below).

Sensory storage

As mentioned in Chapter 1, the sensory storage is primarily a filter for a variety of sensory inputs. If you think about it for a moment, all our senses are constantly bombarded by environmental information. As you are reading this book, your body is receiving information from all your senses. Most of this information is not retained for any longer than fractions of a second. However, a small proportion is kept and transferred into STM. Lloyd (1984) estimated that only 1/20 of sensory memories are translated into more lasting representations. Sensory storage is therefore the 'gatekeeper' of what information goes on to be processed further and what is

'lost'. Once external inputs are selected, they are passed to STM.

Features of STM

As we have already seen in Chapter 1, STM is a concept that has been around in different ways for well over a hundred years. When Atkinson and Shiffrin incorporated it into their model, they proposed it had a number of features. Perhaps the most important of these is that through rehearsal, information may be transferred from STM to LTM (see Figure 2.1 below).

Rehearsal

Within their original model, Atkinson and Shiffrin believed that the longer information was held in STM or the number of repetitions were the 'key' to whether information was transferred to LTM.

Studies by researchers such as Craik and Watkins (1973) argue that neither of these criteria are impor-

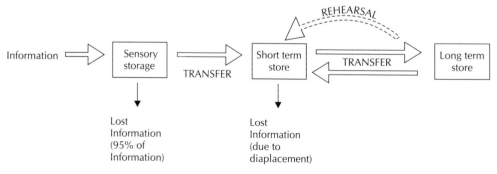

Figure 2.1: Multi-store model.

tant as predictors of whether information becomes transferred to long term storage. Craik and Watkins went on to suggest that in actual fact there are two types of rehearsal:

- maintenance, and
- elaborative.

Maintenance rehearsal involves purely repeating the material over and over again. This is the technique often used by actors to learn their lines. Elaborative rehearsal involves 'doing something with' the material as you are repeating it – for example, making associations with existing knowledge. So for Craik and Watkins it wasn't rehearsal *per se* that was important, but the type of rehearsal.

Primacy and recency effects

In Chapter 1 we looked at various methods of recall. One of these is known as free recall. This involves allowing people to retrieve information in whichever order they wish. The best way to achieve this is to give people a blank sheet of paper and ask them to write down their responses.

A striking feature of the free recall method was discovered back in 1962 by a researcher called Murdock. He coined the phrase 'serial position effect' to describe it. People tend to remember what appeared at the beginning of a list (primacy effect) and at the end (recency effect). What appeared in the middle is more than likely to be forgotten. Interestingly, nearly all of Murdock's participants remembered the last word.

Glanzer and Cunitz (1966) explained the 'serial position effect' in terms of the STM/LTM dichotomy. They argued that the reason we remember more at the beginning of a list is because these have had the chance to be stored in LTM. The reason we remember more at the end is because they are still in STM. The information in the middle, in a sense, is in 'limbo'; it doesn't transfer to LTM and quickly fades from STM.

Glanzer and Cunitz also found that when participants were not allowed to rehearse, after about 30 seconds (the duration of STM) the recency effect disappeared, but the primacy effect remained.

Type of encoding in STM

Most of the early work into how information was encoded into STM suggested it to be acoustic – that is, through sound. Conrad (1962, 1964) found that when participants made errors in their STM recall, often the letters they got wrong sounded the same – for example, 'b' was confused for 'd', or 'p' for 't'. Studies such as these led to speculation that the STM mode of encoding was primarily acoustic.

Capacity and duration of STM

Chapter 1 cites the work of George Miller (1956) and his ideas regarding 'chunking' (see page 10). Atkinson and Shiffrin proposed that STM was limited in terms of its storage capacity to approximately seven items. Other studies have also shown the number seven to be important.

Within the area of social cognition, Mischel (1968) found that people gave approximately seven personality traits when describing individuals they had just met. It appeared that this was roughly the limit of social characteristics that could be held in STM.

Studies from other cultures seem to suggest that this 'magic number seven' is a robust finding. For example, Yu *et al* (1985) found that Chinese speakers were able to hold approximately seven (plus or minus two) characters within their STM. Atkinson and Shiffrin proposed we can hold information in STM for approximately 30 seconds (if unrehearsed).

Thinking and STM

Everyday thinking involves STM. If someone asks you to solve a simple maths problem you need to be able to retain the numbers, carry out the calculation and store the final answer. Some researchers argue that all everyday problem-solving involves STM (for example Ericsson and Simon, 1984).

Giving people the right change involves remembering how much money something cost. Reading instructions on how to set up a video recorder requires recalling information you read a few seconds ago. Writing an essay requires you to remember what was said at the beginning of a sentence. Even Mischel's study (mentioned above) shows that personality attributions are limited to how much we can store in STM.

Features of LTM

Many researchers argue that there are different types of LTM (see Chapter 1). Tulving (1972) suggested there were procedural, semantic and episodic memories. One of the problems with Atkinson and Shiffrin's model is that they didn't differentiate between the types of LTM. They saw it as a permanent storage with an unlimited capacity.

Commentary

- There has been considerable experimental research conducted on the multi-store model. Some of it appears to confirm the existence of short and long term storage.

- Work within clinical psychology also appears to give weight to the idea that STM and LTM are separate systems. As will be seen in more detail in Chapter 4, HM suffered from amnesia (memory loss). His STM was fine, but he couldn't transfer new information into LTM (Milner *et al*, 1978).

- One of the major criticisms of the multi-store model is its concept that rehearsal is the vital factor in transferring information from short to long term memory. Researchers such as Jenkins (1974) argue that it's not the rehearsal itself that is important, but what we do to the information.

- These ideas led to the development of a new approach – one that doesn't require memory to be divided up into compartments, but instead focuses on the processing of material.

Levels of processing model

As an alternative idea to the multi-store model, Fergus Craik and Robert Lockhart (1972) proposed their levels of processing model (see Figure 2.2).

They argued that rather than viewing memory as a 'structural' phenomenon (with short and long term stores), it should be viewed as a 'process' – in other words, it's not where information goes that describes memory, it's what we do with it.

Their viewpoint was that information we process in a limited way is fragile and temporary (their equivalent to Atkinson and Shiffrin's STM). Remembering a telephone number is artificial and mechanistic. We do not usually make any 'deep and meaningful' associations with a random selection of numbers. However, when we want to remember something in a permanent way we will expend much more 'cognitive effort', and will process this information in a more meaningful way (their equivalent to Atkinson and Shiffrin's LTM).

In RLA 15 (see Chapter 4, page 44), employees at the finance company Lombard Finance have brought meaning to their telephone number by relating it to the value of the company's loans. The amounts start from £800 and go up to £15,000. Their telephone number is 0800 2 15000. This is a really good example of creating 'deeper processing'.

So how much information can we process, and is it of a particular type?

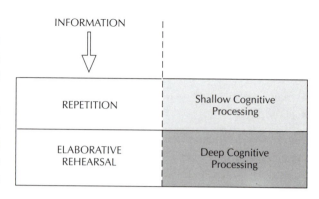

Figure 2.2: Levels of processing model

The Stroop effect

There are studies which show that people process more information than they are always consciously aware of. A good example of this is the Stroop effect (Stroop, 1935). The study commonly involves asking people to name the colour of ink a word is written in. Participants are usually quicker if the colour and the word are the same – for example, if the word 'red' is written in red ink or the word 'blue' is written in blue ink.

Even though the explanation for this is not fully understood, it appears that processing of colour and word meaning (semantics) are occurring simultaneously without being prompted. We perhaps process more information than we are aware of.

Persistent findings such as these encouraged Craik and Lockhart to revise their model in 1975. They added that all stimuli undergo a basic level of semantic analysis – something they called 'minimal core encoding'.

Levels of processing and rehearsal

In their original model, Craik and Lockhart (1972) distinguished between two distinct types of rehearsal (or processing):

- type I, and
- type II.

Type I was defined as maintenance rehearsal – nothing more than repetition or rote learning (how actors might learn lines in a play). Type II was defined as elaborative rehearsal – a more complex, deeper level of processing. Their argument was the more you allowed people to 'process' the material, the better it would be remembered. A major problem with this, though, is working out what constitutes 'deep' or 'shallow' processing.

Elaboration and distinctiveness

Anderson and Reder (1979) suggested that one of the main reasons why elaborative rehearsal allowed 'deeper processing' was because it facilitated elaboration. If, in a list, we could bring 'personal meaning' to certain words, the chances are those words would be recalled more easily. For example, if one of the words was 'Torquay' and you had been there on holiday, it would have personal significance for you. On encoding you would be associating it with past experiences.

One of the earliest studies to look at elaborative rehearsal was conducted by Craik and Tulving (1975). They asked participants to complete either 'elaborated' or 'non-elaborated' sentences. Participants were then unexpectedly asked to recall the words they had previously submitted.

What they found was that even though both tasks had involved a high level of cognitive input, the elaborated sentences produced better recall. This illustrates that it isn't just depth of processing that is important, but the level to which we elaborate the material.

Taking this idea a stage further, researchers such as Eysenck (1979), suggested that the more distinctive the elaborations, the more likely it is that material will be remembered.

Eysenck (1984) went on to say that 'distinctiveness' is a very difficult concept to define. A word may only be distinctive to us for highly personal reasons. The word 'baby' might not mean anything to you, but for me, it may hold deep significance and therefore be very distinctive.

Commentary

The real problem is that levels of processing, elaboration and distinctiveness are so interrelated, that it is almost impossible to identify them separately (Eysenck, 1993).

Levels of processing and facial recognition

Bower and Karlin (1974) attempted to apply the levels of processing model to the recognition of faces. They found that when they encouraged participants to encode at a 'deeper level' by getting them to rate the faces for characteristics such as honesty and so on, recall was higher than shallow processing (getting participants to identify whether faces were male or female). But researchers such as Intraub and Nickolos (1985) question these effects. They argue that 'distinctiveness', not the levels of processing, determines better memory. However,

the two are interrelated. The more you 'look' (or process) a face, the more distinctions you will identify.

Commentary

- This was seen as a useful model because it related memory to our other cognitive systems. It focused on how we give meaning to information, and related that to ease of recall.
- However, some researchers believe that the model fails to address crucial issues such as why deeper processing should improve memory (Eysenck and Keane 1995). It therefore becomes a descriptive model rather than explaining why.

The working memory model

Another approach to understanding memory was proposed by Baddeley and Hitch (1974) and Hitch and Baddeley (1976). Their model focused on STM. They felt that the 'multi-stage' model's unitary approach to STM was too simplistic.

Their belief was that encoding in STM was a highly complex procedure that required different 'types of processing'. Within their model, they suggested that STM comprised three separate components. There was a central executive that acted as an attentional system. Second, they described a system called the 'articulatory loop' and third, a 'visuo-spatial scratch pad'. Later, Baddeley and Lewis (1982) added a fourth component, a 'primary acoustic store'. We will now consider these in more detail (see Figure 2.3 below).

The central executive

This component was proposed as the 'gatekeeper' to all information entering the mind ready for processing. It directs information to the other systems and

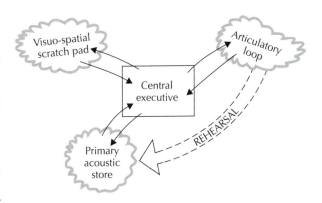

Figure 2.3: The working memory model

integrates their responses. It is limited in its storage and, because of its overall directing role, can process information in any sensory form. Because it is only 'attending' to data and then deciding what should be done with it, it can viewed as a 'pure attentional system' (Baddeley, 1981).

Hunt (1980), found that when participants were given a 'dual task' (doing two things simultaneously), the performance of one task was affected by the other. Evidence such as this could imply that the central executive is unable to deal with two 'strands' of information simultaneously, and therefore performance on one will suffer. This suggests that all information passes through the central executive before being sent to its respective processing component.

The articulatory loop

This is a very similar idea to Atkinson and Shiffrin's notion of rehearsal. When we attempt to remember something in STM, we repeat it out loud – often a number of times. This repetition reinforces the material.

The term 'loop' is actually quite useful in describing how information is repeated over and over again. But what are the limitations of the articulatory loop? According to Baddeley et al (1975) it is limited to what a person can articulate (say out loud) in approximately two seconds. Also, it appears that it can only process one piece of phonological (sound) information at a time. This concept is referred to as 'articulatory suppression'.

Wilding and Mohindra (1980) carried out a dual-task procedure and found that if they asked people to carry out an articulatory suppression task (in this study, repeating the word 'the'), their subsequent memory recall was impaired. The task of repeating the word 'the' had interfered with the participants' ability to use the articulatory loop.

Visuo-spatial scratch pad

Not all information we encode is phonological. Often, it takes the form of visual or spatial material. In 1980, Baddeley and Lieberman reinforced the distinction between visual and spatial information. They proposed that we are better at remembering the position of information (spatial details) than the information itself (visual imagery). However, the 'scratch pad' is able to deal with 'pictorial information' as well.

As RLA 9 shows (see page 26), imagery plays a very important role in the retrieval of information.

'Mental pictures' are held in the 'visuo-spatial scratch pad'.

One widely used technique that utilizes this idea is the 'method of loci' (Wollen et al, 1972). A person imagines a familiar house, then he or she associates items they wish to remember with certain rooms. The more bizarre the associations, the more likely they are to be remembered. The person then visualizes him/herself walking through the house. If the process is successful, the person will recall the items associated with each room.

The primary acoustic store

Baddeley and Hitch's original model did not include an acoustic store; it was added later by Baddeley and Lewis. A slightly earlier study had suggested the need for an acoustic store. Baddeley and Lewis (1981) asked participants to make judgements on whether or not visually presented 'nonsense' words sounded like actual words. An example would be the word 'cayoss'.

An articulatory suppression exercise did not affect the performance on this task, indicating that participants were utilising another memory component other than the articulatory loop. They proposed this was the primary acoustic store. According to Hitch (1980), this component is primarily involved in retaining recently heard speech.

Commentary

- The studies examined suggest that this more detailed approach to STM is much more realistic in explaining how memory works in everyday life.
- However, one of the problems of the model is that most of the evidence has been produced within the laboratory. We could argue that it lacks exactly what it claims to explain – namely, memory in everyday settings.

Schema theory

Schema's can be defined as 'mental representations'. Within the context of memory they usually refer to the process of using existing knowledge to interpret new information (Cohen, 1993).

Bartlett (1932) first used the term to explain how we 'construct' memories from existing knowledge (see Chapter 1). He suggested that we attempt to make 'efforts after meaning'.

Many psychological theories refer to 'bottom-up' and 'top-down' processing when discussing schema theory. The idea behind these descriptions is that we use 'top-down' processing (based on existing information) to interpret 'bottom-up' information – that is, new material acquired from the outside world.

Bartlett's stories

Sir Frederic Bartlett (1932) published the findings of his work in a classic book entitled *Remembering*. Typically, his research involved presenting participants with short stories, which they had to recall at a later date.

One of the most published of these stories is 'The war of the ghosts' (see page 24), an American Indian folk tale. It tells the story of two American Indians who join a raiding party. One of the Indians is wounded in the ensuing battle and brought back home.

Because the story is not taken from Western culture, it contains a number of unusual descriptions. There are many references to ghosts and the death scene of the injured Indian is outlined as follows.

When the sun rose, he fell down. Something black came out of his mouth. His face became contorted. The people jumped up and cried. He was dead.

Most of the British subjects found the story difficult to understand. They were interpreting it within their existing knowledge (schemas). Most of them, in later reproductions, missed out the references to the ghosts altogether. This and other alterations to the story led Bartlett to propose that we adapt information to suit our preconceptions. Ghosts tend not to be central to Western experiences. Therefore, they were not actively remembered.

There have been other studies that have given support to Bartlett's ideas. For example, Bower *et al* (1979) found that when participants read a short passage about characters in a restaurant, later they recalled information that had not appeared in the original passage. This 'created' information was based on their pre-existing schemas regarding restaurants. Participants would often talk about eating behaviours or how the meal was paid for, even though none of these were mentioned in the original story.

How does schema theory apply to memory?

It appears that schema theory applies to both the encoding and retrieval of memories. Brewer and Nakamura (1984) suggest that existing schemas can influence how we search for existing information, thereby directly affecting the type of search we begin. Cohen (1986) suggests there are a number of

ways in which schema's affect memory. These are outlined below.

Memory selection

First, they could affect what information we attend to. Our existing schemas may suggest that certain information is irrelevant. This may be ignored when encoding. We may be able to remember an amount of money someone paid us. However, it is unlikely we would be able to remember the colour of the ink with which he or she wrote the cheque. The actual amount was part of a bigger schema inside our mind, the ink colour wasn't.

Generalization of memories

Second, material tends to become more general when we try to recall it. If we try to re-tell a story that has been told to us, often we miss out specific details; we tend to remember only the general meaning. This is true of 'gossip'. Due to the fact that many people are involved in the transfer of this sort of 'story-telling', the facts become more and more general until it becomes difficult to know what information comes from the original story and what comes from the 'storyteller's' imagination.

Making sense of new information

Third, we interpret new information using our existing schemas, then encode both the information and our interpretation of it. A number of excellent examples of this are discussed in Chapter 4. Most of the research into eyewitness testimony suggests that it is highly unreliable because of the high level of personal interpretation.

Expectations

Fourth, in a similar way our expectations of what we believe 'should have happened' affect how we recall information. These expectations are frequently based on stereotypes.

Howitt (1991) presented a passage of text to participants, then later asked them to recall it. The text had been written in such a way as to allow ambiguous racial interpretation. In many cases participants showed racist bias in their recall. Even though many of the participants believed themselves to not be racist at the start of the study, their recall suggested they were.

Sulin and Dooling (1974) conducted a similar study. Participants were asked to read a passage about a dictator. In one condition they were given a fictitious name; in the other they were told the dictator was Adolf Hitler. Later they were asked if the passage had contained the line: 'He hated the Jews particularly and so persecuted them.' Even though this line was not in the passage, those who were told the dictator was Adolf Hitler believed this line to be in the original text.

As mentioned before, one of the most common applications where stereotypes can have serious implications is within the legal system. Identifying criminals in 'line-ups' or compiling 'photofit' faces are more than often distorted to fit our expectations of what we believe a criminal looks like.

Real Life Application 8:
Schema theory and criminal faces

Material A: A case of mistaken identity

Dr Robert Shomer, an American forensic expert, advertises his services on the Internet. His web page is dedicated to wrongful convictions that he suggests are primarily caused by mistaken identifications. Over the past 25 years, Dr Shomer has testified as an expert witness in eyewitness identi-

their book *The social psychology of facial appearance* (1988), researchers Bull and Rumsey suggest that many people are quite confident about identifying criminals by their appearance alone. The book suggests that many people have a stereotypical view of what a criminal looks like.

Material C: What criminals look like

Back in 1876, Cesare Lombroso believed it was possible to identify a criminal by a number of facial features. He described male criminals as

 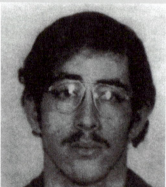 

fication in over 250 trials, in numerous American states. Above is one example he gives of mistaken identity. You can see how easily mistakes can occur in facial recognition.

'That's the man!
I'll never forget that face!'

The men on the left and right were picked out of police line-ups by victims of rapes and robberies committed by the man in the middle.

Article adapted from www.eyewitnessid.com

Material B: Eyewitness testimony – remembering faces

Psychologists such as Professor Graham Davies, an expert in eyewitness research, have argued for many years for a change in the law to prevent people being convicted on the basis of identification alone (1994). Davies argues people tend to remember faces very poorly and recall using their 'stereotyped' knowledge (or schemas). In fact, in

having 'enormous jaws', high cheek bones, prominent eyebrow ridges and 'handle-shaped' ears. The Victorian criminologist Havelock Ellis also identified 'typical criminal types' (see illustrations on page 23).

Material D: Using existing knowledge to recall faces

It could be argued that these stereotyped images of criminals are still presented today in film portrayals of 'the bad guy', all of which serves to reinforce our 'mental image' of the face of a criminal. This notion of attempting to remember a face by fitting it into an existing schema (even if it is a stereotype) was first explained by Bartlett in 1932 in his theory of 'efforts after meaning' (see page 21). People want their memories to make sense, so they use pre-conceived ideas to help 'shape' the recall. On many occasions this means that accuracy is sacrificed.

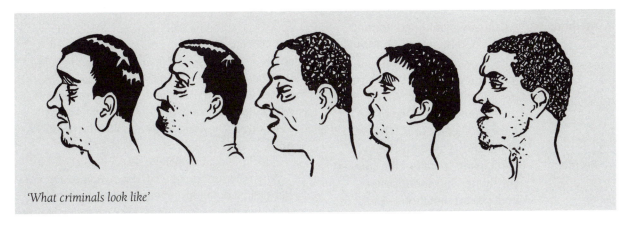

'What criminals look like'

Summary

- Many people are poor at remembering faces. This is highly problematic when legal cases require accurate eyewitness testimony.
- Bull and Rumsey propose we judge people to be criminal based on their appearance.
- Lombroso suggested criminals had certain facial features. Ironically his descriptions only applied to men!
- Even today, the media use stereotypes to portray 'criminals'. The general public will often say: 'He looks like a "baddy".'

Questions

1 What are the problems with using existing knowledge when retrieving memories?

2 Discuss the roles of 'stereotypes' in cases of mistaken identity.

Expert knowledge

Everything discussed so far regarding schema theory has been based on Bartlett's original assertion that memories are based on our existing knowledge. But what if we are 'expert' within a particular field?

Spilich *et al* (1979) conducted an experiment in which they compared participants who had a great knowledge of baseball with those who did not. All the participants listened to a five-minute commentary of a baseball match. In a free recall situation, those participants who had greater knowledge recalled significantly more information and made fewer errors in reporting events that had occurred during the match. It was as if:

'for the people who knew little or nothing about baseball, memorising the commentary was like learning nonsense material' (Cohen, 1989).

A similar finding was obtained by Chase and Simon (1973) when they compared the memories of three chess players: a novice, an expert and a master. Not surprisingly, the master's ability to reconstruct a stage of a match was far superior when compared to the other two.

Perhaps we should be careful that we don't assume expert knowledge leads to better memory. It is much more likely that having knowledge about a subject allows the person to make more sense of material, and therefore organize it into groups, thereby making it more retrievable (Cohen, 1989).

Commentary

- Bartlett's contribution to memory research was pioneering. He was the first to suggest that memory was an active, constructive process, and that existing beliefs, knowledge and so on are just as important to consider as the process of memory itself.
- As will be seen in Chapter 4, schema theory is a very useful starting point to improve memorability in many real life settings. If we begin by asking how people will interpret this new information based on what they already know, we can decide how to focus and organize the information we wish them to remember.
- One of the major criticisms of schema theory is the fact it is very vague (Cohen, 1993).

KEY STUDY 3

Researcher: Bartlett (1932)

Aims: Using a variety of stories, the aim was to illustrate that memory is an active process, dependent on individual interpretation.

Method:	As already mentioned, Bartlett used a number of stories (or folk tales) from other cultures, making it difficult for Western participants to understand fully their significance. One of the most cited of these is 'The war of the ghosts' (see box below).
Results:	Participants' recall of the story got shorter and shorter after multiple presentations. After about six presentations it had been reduced from 330 words to 180. Participants frequently attributed their own interpretation. For example, the reference to the canoe was often changed (by Western participants) to a boat.
Conclusions:	Memory is influenced by our existing knowledge, which in turn is created by the culture in which we live.

The war of the ghosts

One night, two young men from Egulac went down to the river to hunt seals, and while they were there it became foggy and calm. Then they heard war-cries, and they thought: 'Maybe this is a war-party.' They escaped to the shore, and hid behind a log.

Now canoes came up, and they heard the noise of paddles and saw one canoe coming up to them. There were five men in the canoe and they said: 'What do you think? We wish to take you along. We are going up the river to make war on the people.'

One of the young men said: 'I have no arrows.'

'Arrows are in the canoe,' they said.

'I will not go along. I might be killed. My relatives do not know where I have gone. But you,' he said turning to the other, 'may go with them.'

So one of the young men went, but the other returned home. And the warriors went on up the river to a town on the other side of Kalama. The people came down to the water and began to fight, and many were killed. But presently, one of the young men heard one of the warriors say: 'Quick, let us go home. That Indian has been hit.'

Now he thought: 'Oh, they are ghosts.' He did not feel sick, but he had been shot. So the canoes went back to Egulac, and the young man went ashore to his house and made a fire. And he told everybody and said: 'Behold, I accompanied the ghosts, and we went to fight. Many of our fellows were killed and many of those who attacked us were killed. They said I was hit, but I did not feel sick.'

He told it all, and then he became quiet.

When the sun rose, he fell down. Something black came out of his mouth. His face became contorted. The people jumped up and cried. He was dead.

Source: Bartlett, (1932)

Organizational models of memory and imagery

In schema theory, people fit new information into existing thoughts. Clearly if material could be organized in a 'helpful' way, it could be integrated into existing knowledge more effectively. For this reason, many memory theorists have concentrated on the way in which material is presented. Meyer (1973) stated: 'To remember is to have organized.' As we will see in Chapter 4, this concept has many applications. It may be possible to get your patients or clients to remember something more effectively by manipulating the way in which you present it.

Hierarchical network model

In 1969, Allan Collins and Ross Quillian published a paper outlining their 'cognitive economy model' of human memory. Their research was based on participants understanding information, and for this reason it is often referred to as a 'semantic network model'. They based it on a simple computer analogy. They proposed that information is stored in a 'hierarchical network'. This network is made up of different levels, which each represent categories of information. From these we have interconnections that link ideas together (see Figure 2.4 on page 25). People were asked general knowledge questions such as: 'Do birds fly?' or 'Can a canary sing?'.

In order to test their model, Collins and Quillian developed a true/false test, which was timed. They found it took participants longer to answer questions that required 'travelling down more paths' on the hierarchy than those which did not.

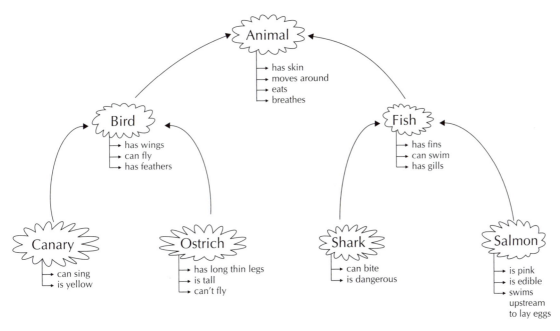

Figure 2.4: Collins and Quillian's hierarchical network model

The 'spreading activation concept'

This idea of a hierarchical network has been taken further by Medin and Ross (1992) in their idea about spreading activation. They argue that when we access a particular concept, we also stimulate a whole 'neural network'. In a physiological sense, we activate related pathways.

This is often used as an explanation of why we describe experiencing a 'train of thought'. If certain ideas happen to share part of a network, we can often activate them at the same time. An example of this might be as follows. While shopping in the supermarket, you notice a drink that you enjoyed while on holiday a few years ago. This stimulates memories of the beach, the hot weather and that special person you met. Seeing the bottle has set in motion a stream of memories all closely related in terms of their network proximity.

How does organization take place?

Sometimes in a memory experiment, participants impose an organization themselves when attempting to learn a list of words. This is often referred to as subject-based organization (SO). Clearly the experimenter can do nothing about this, as people will bring to bear their own personal experiences in how they group the material. If the experimenter deliberately sets out the material to be learnt in a particular way, this is referred to as experimenter-based organization (EO).

A classic EO study carried out by Bower *et al* (1969) presented participants with either an organized hierarchical word list or a random one (see RLA 9, page 26). Participants recalled significantly more words from the organized list than the random list. This sort of study shows that by imposing a 'logical structure' to a group of words, we can enhance memory recall. The next question is *why?*

In essence the answer can be found in schema theory. By organising information into logical groups, we are making it fit into existing schemas and thereby enhancing its memorabilty. Baddeley (1995) suggests that organization helps us to:

'integrate and relate [new information] to what is already known'.

Commentary

- A lot of useful research has focused on the effects of organization on memory. It has useful applications within the real world (see Ley *et al*'s work in Chapter 4 as an example).

- However, there are two cautionary points. First, as with a lot of research, most studies within this area took place within the laboratory, working with rather 'dull' word lists. To what extent we can generalize the findings to everyday experiences is questionable. Second, organization within memory is a highly focused area, and any theories generated will be limited in what they can explain.

Real Life Application 9:

Organization in memory

Bower *et al* (1969) conducted a study in which they gave participants a list of 112 words to remember. In one condition, participants were presented with 28 words over four trials. These words were arranged into a logical hierarchy (see Figure 2.5 below). In the other condition, once again 28 words were presented over four trials – except these words were not organized but randomly presented. Participants in the organized condition recalled significantly more words out of the 112 than participants in the unorganized condition.

Organization using hierarchies can be very useful in real life situations (see Chapter 4) when complex or large quantities of material need to be retained.

Summary

- Bowers' study shows that presenting material in an organized, logical way facilitates retention.
- Techniques such as 'hierarchies' can be used when presenting complex or large quantities of material.

Questions

1 Using your knowledge of memory theories, why should organising material into hierarchies improve retention?

2 What are the problems with laboratory studies conducted into memory, such as Bowers'?

KEY STUDY 4

Researchers:	Bower, Cark, Lesgold and Winzenz (1969)
Aims:	This study attempted to test the notion that organising words into a logical hierarchy will improve recall.
Method:	Two groups of participants were asked to learn 112 words. In one condition the words were organized into logical hierarchies and 28 words were presented over four trials. In the second condition, 28 words were presented over four trials, except this time they were presented randomly (no organization was imposed).
Results:	The mean average score for the hierarchy group was 73, whereas the mean score for the random condition was 21.
Conclusions:	By organising words into a logical hierarchy, memory recall was significantly improved.

Imagery

Allan Paivio (1969) was one of the earliest researchers to study scientifically the effects of imagery on memory recall. In his early work he demonstrated that 'concrete' words (ones that can generate a pictorial representation) were better recalled than 'abstract' words (ones that are very difficult to picture). The word 'tree' would have a better chance of being remembered than a word such as 'loyalty'.

Bower (1970) took the importance of imagery further by suggesting that material that was made to

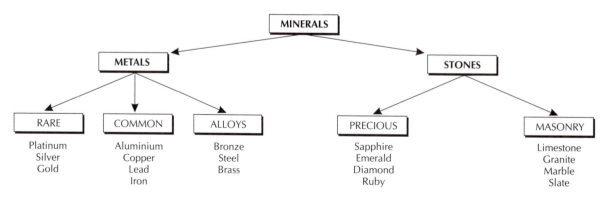

Figure 2.5: Hierarchies as a form of organisation

'interact' is more likely to be remembered than material that is just paired together. If we were trying to remember the words 'doll', 'chair' and 'flag', we could picture a doll standing on a chair waving a flag. This, according to Bower, is more likely to be recalled than just picturing the three items side by side. It also appears that the more bizarre we make the associations or images, the more likely the items are to be recalled (Anderson, 1995).

In RLA 5 (Chapter 1, page 12) we looked at mnemonic methods for improving recall. The 'word link' system uses rhyming 'images' as a framework to attach new material to – for example, 1 = bun, 2 = shoe, 3 = tree and so on. If we were trying to remember three Christmas presents for our friends (a watch, a book and a CD), we could make the following links.

1 A watch wrapped around a bun.

2 A shoe sticking out of a book (like a book mark).

3 A tree with CDs hanging from the branches.

Commentary

- As with organization, because this is only one very narrow aspect of memory, any findings gained from research conducted into this field are limited in how far they can be generalized.
- As individuals often create their own mental pictures or images, it is difficult to control this within experimental research.

Physiological explanations of memory

As seen in Chapter 1, Hebb was the first investigator to propose a physiological underpinning for memory. Since his work, many researchers have looked at this link. Some have attempted to identify areas of the brain associated with memory formation and storage. More recently, others have looked at the chemical nature of memories, trying to deduce what bio-chemical changes occur when memories are formed. We will now look at some of these theories.

Structures of the brain associated with memory

Over the years, many different structures have become associated with memories. Some of the early work within this field was pioneered by researchers such as Penfield (1937) and Lashley (1930s and 1940s).

Penfield conducted surgical procedures on patients while they were awake, and by electrically stimulating their brain he was able to identify emotional memories and experiences as the patients reported them. He suggested certain regions of the cortex were involved in certain experiences.

Later in the 1930s and 1940s, investigators such as Karl Lashley attempted to identify electrical activity in certain areas of the brain to try to demonstrate that memories were electrical in nature and took place in certain areas. Unfortunately his work was unsuccessful.

The current view

Today, most contemporary neuroscientists are of the opinion that the brain has specialized regions involved in memory formation and general areas for long term storage (McCarthy, 1995). Certain areas have been shown to be involved in specialized functions. For example, the temporal lobes are believed to be where some long term memories are permanently stored.

The hippocampus is proposed to be involved in the formation and retrieval of memories. In fact, this structure is seen as the 'control centre' of our memory, collecting and cross-referencing inputs from all our sensory modalities (see Figure 2.6 below).

The amygdala is believed to house our unconscious experiences, while the caudate nucleus is involved in 'instinctual' evolutionary-type memories. As mentioned earlier, memory involves 'networks' within the whole of the brain, not just spe-

cific areas. For example, if we were to close our eyes and recall someone we know, this action would require visual regions of the brain providing us with that information. The same would be true for recalling melodies to our favourite songs. Auditory regions of the brain would need to be involved.

Smell (olfaction) as a trigger for memories

People have long observed that smells can trigger powerful memories. Perhaps you have had the experience of catching the 'whiff' of some aroma that you haven't been exposed to for many years. Within seconds, floods of memories pour into your conscious and you are transported back in time. Scientists can now explain why this is. The part of the brain that detects taste and smell (the lateral olfactory area) is very close anatomically to the part of the brain responsible for memory (the hippocampus) (see Figure 2.7 on page 29). From an evolutionary perspective, it makes sense to have a good memory for smells. We remember, and hopefully avoid, things that smell unpleasant. They could be potentially dangerous.

Commentary

- As mentioned earlier, one of the problems with using the biological approach in the study of memory is the temptation to assume that individual structures of the brain relate to specific aspects of memory. Even

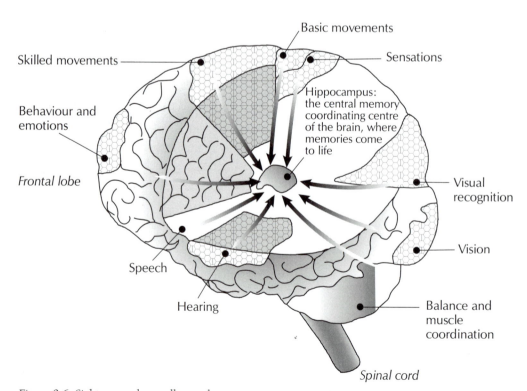

Figure 2.6: Sight + sound + smell = good memory

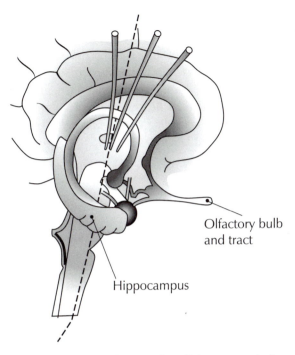

Olfactory bulb and tract

Hippocampus

Figure 2.7: Location of taste and smell detectors in the brain

though certain anatomical regions do appear to have key roles, the processing of memories involves the whole brain.

- Biological studies in memory are primarily conducted on animals within laboratories. This throws into doubt how useful such an approach is in explaining real life, human memory experiences.

The bio-chemical nature of memory

Much of the contemporary work into memory has focused not so much on structures within the brain as on *processes*. Changes at a cellular level are thought to be at the heart of memory formation.

An early study within this area was conducted by Kandel and Schwartz (1982). They studied the common sea snail (aplysia) and found that learning was accompanied by an increase in the secretion of a brain chemical (neurotransmitter) called acetylcholine. Incidentally, the neurotransmitter acetylcholine has been implicated within Alzheimer's disease (see Chapter 4). One of the main characteristics of this degenerative illness is loss of memory. Some studies have shown that drugs which increase acetylcholine production also improve memory (Bartus *et al*, 1982).

Nootropics: drugs that improve memory

Does this mean, therefore, that it is possible to design drugs that enhance memory? One of the problems with drugs that use acetylcholine is that it is found throughout the body and it has more functions than just regulating memory. Any drug would have to select only acetylcholine receptors that related to memory function.

Recently, Winkler and colleagues (1995) had some success in genetically modifying acetylcholine cells. The brain was the target and brain-damaged laboratory animals showed some improvement of memory. But acetylcholine is not the only substance that is believed to improve memory.

Real Life Application 10:

'Smart drugs' – drugs that enhance memory

Many pharmaceutical companies are investing heavily in what have become known as 'smart drugs' (substances that apparently improve or enhance cognitive functioning, including memory). A new family of drugs called ampakines, which have developed in the USA, can help rats remember their way around a maze and help young men with 'normal' memories perform up to 20 per cent better in tests of short term recall.

However, some researchers, such as Dr John Kerr at the University of Surrey, question the validity of such drugs.

In many cases the 'placebo effect' is very strong, and controlled trials have produced no evidence that these drugs can enhance mental function.

Regardless of the debates, many drugs and substances are proposed to enhance cognitive abilities (they are correctly referred to as nootropics). These chemicals include piracetam, vincamine and hydergine. Phenytoin, a drug commonly prescribed for epilepsy, has been shown to increase IQ and long term memory in normal, healthy young and elderly volunteers. Vasopressin, a hormone secreted by the pituitary gland, has been found to improve concentration, attention and memory. Even herbal substances such as ginkgo biloba (extracted from the maidenhair tree) have been shown to possess nootropic powers.

Extract adapted from the *Guardian*, 11 February 1997

Summary

- Many companies are investing money into the development of nootropics (drugs that can enhance cognitive abilities, including memory).
- Not all academics are convinced that these drugs are as effective as some claim. The placebo effect has been cited as a factor that may be 'interfering' with any of the positive results found.
- Many substances have been suggested as having nootropic effects. Some of these include drugs such as piracetam, hydergine and phenytoin. Naturally occurring substances such as the hormone vasopressin and the herb ginkgo biloba have also been implicated.

Questions

1 Identify the possible benefits and problems of nootropics.

2 In your own words, explain the proposed role of acetylcholine within memory.

Factors that can affect memory

Because of the chemical nature of memory, many factors can interfere with the physiology of consolidation. In the text below we will briefly consider three factors:

- alcohol
- dieting, and
- hormone replacement therapy (HRT).

The effect of alcohol on memory

Alcohol 'sedates' the central nervous system and slows down communication between nerve cells. For this reason, temporary interference occurs in the consolidation of memories, when a person is under the influence of alcohol.

Ironically, if the person had not consumed large quantities of alcohol, then one of the best ways to 'retrieve' memories encoded while being drunk is to get drunk again. This is an example of 'context dependent learning' (see Chapter 1).

Long term alcohol abuse can lead to a deficiency in vitamin B1 (thiamine) and, eventually, possibly to Korsakoff's syndrome (see Chapter 4).

Memory and dieting

Women who go on crash diets [that is, diets that claim to result in a rapid weight loss] run the risk of lowering their intelligence, a scientist warned yesterday. They are likely to suffer significant 'mental impairment', becoming more forgetful than hearty eaters and displaying slower reactions, according to Dr Michael Green, a research scientist at Unilever Research.

Extract adapted from the
Daily Express newspaper, September 1999.

Hormones and memory

Some recent research has suggested that oestrogen can give women's memories a real boost. Barbara Sherwin (1999) proposes that women deprived of oestrogen suffer from memory lapses. These lapses disappear when the hormone is replaced.

Previous studies have focused on the importance of oestrogen as a 'cognitive enhancer'. In July 1999, *New scientist* reported that mental ability is linked to oestrogen exposure in the womb. Also, recent studies have suggested that hormone replacement therapy (HRT), can help to protect post-menopausal women from memory diseases such as Alzheimer's.

The synapse: the place where memory takes place

More recent ideas have suggested that it is not so much the neuro-chemicals themselves that are important, but the connections between nerve cells (neurons).

Collingridge (1997) has suggested that memory formation takes place where neurons meet (referred to as synapses). If a single neuron becomes highly active (a process called long term potentiation), it does not mean that all the other cells also become 'excited'. This single cell may well excite other neurons further down the network, not necessarily at its own synapse. The fact that neurons can work independently suggests memories are not always stored within close proximity to one another.

Real Life Application 11:
The physiology of memory

Back in the late 1940s, a Canadian psychologist called Donald Hebb suggested that the repeated 'firing' of neurones (nerve cells) would make the connections between cells in the brain stronger.

Ironically, over 50 years earlier, William James

(1890), in his famous book *Principles of psychology*, suggested a very similar idea for behaviours of habit. He proposed that repeating a behaviour strengthened its pathway in the nervous system, hence leading to an 'ease of repeatability' (what we might commonly call a habit). He referred to this strengthening as 'plasticity'.

Both Hebb and James were on the right lines according to modern neuroscientists. A widely held view regarding the formation of memories is explained by a concept known as 'long term potentiation' (LTP). In simple terms, chemical markers released between nerve cells, link nerve cell networks together. The more these networks are used, the more efficiently individual nerve cells will link with one another. This network formation and usage is what we call memory.

Article adapted from *Focus* magazine, March 1994.

Summary

- The idea of 'strengthening' connections between neurons as the basis of memory was originally proposed by people such as James and Hebb.
- Modern neuroscientists call this strengthening long term potentiation. The more connections are used, the stronger the memory becomes.

Questions

1 In your own words, describe long term potentiation.

2 What are the advantages and disadvantages of studying memory from a biological perspective?

Memory and old age

It is nearly always assumed that as we get older, our memories will deteriorate drastically. In one study conducted by Harris and Sunderland (1981), quite the opposite effect was found. In tests assessing 'memory failure' the younger group of participants (those aged between 20 and 36) experienced significantly more memory failures than the older group aged from 69 to 80.

This sort of evidence suggests that other factors may influence memory deterioration. One such fac-

tor could be general physical health. Indeed, more recently researchers such as Patrick Rabbitt (1994) at Manchester University Age and Cognitive Performance Research Centre, have suggested that there is a link between mental performance and physical health (see RLA 12 below).

Those elderly people who perform best on cognitive tasks (including memory) seem to live the longest. However, the relationship between ageing and memory is not all such good news, and studies that consider forgetting and old age will be outlined in Chapter 3.

Real Life Application 12:

Physical health and memory deterioration
Since 1982, Patrick Rabbitt at Manchester University's Age and Cognitive Performance Research Centre has been studying healthy individuals aged over 50. He and his colleagues were interested to see what effects ageing had on cognitive performance. One finding was that people age at different rates; therefore cognitive performance including memory reduces at different rates. The idea that as we get older our memories fail is partly a myth. There is decline, but this decline is related to other factors – in particular, general physical health.

Article adapted from *Medical Research Council News*, 1994.

Summary

- It is a commonly held view that as we get older our memories will inevitably deteriorate.
- Evidence provided by researchers such as Harris and Sunderland, and Rabbitt suggests that ageing does not necessarily show a drastic decline in memory.
- Rabbitt relates cognitive abilities (including memory) to general physical health. He suggests: 'Those who perform best on cognitive tests seem to live the longest.'

Questions

1 What potential problem is there with Rabitt's assertion that 'those who perform best on cognitive tests seem to live the longest'?

2 By referring to this section, highlight studies that support the idea that ageing and memory loss is *not* inevitable. By referring to the section on ageing in Chapter 3, highlight studies that suggest it is inevitable.

Essay questions

1 Outline and evaluate one theory within memory research.

2 Use experimental evidence to discuss the organization of information on memory (AEB, summer 1989).

3 a Explain the key features of schema theory.

   b How useful is this theory in the understanding of human memory?

3 Theories of forgetting

This chapter considers a range of theories relating to why we forget. Then it goes on to consider some factors that influence forgetting. Next it looks at how emotions affect forgetting. Forgetting and old age are considered, as is the concept of absentmindedness. Finally, we examine briefly individual differences within forgetting. Real Life Applications that are considered are:

- RLA 13: Memories and dreams
- RLA 14: Anxiety, depression and forgetting.

As we have already seen in Chapter 2, researchers use a variety of approaches to investigate memory. Some work within the biological field, reducing memory to its molecular level. Others take a more theoretical perspective, developing models and flow charts. Some look at one specific area of memory, hoping to be able to generalize their findings at a later date. It seems reasonable, then, to find a similar approach in the area of forgetting.

Memory consolidation and trace decay theory

The trace decay theory has its roots within physiology. Researchers such as Hebb (1949; see Chapter 1) suggested that short term exposure to a stimuli only creates 'reverberating' nerve cell activity, and it is not strong or persistent enough to create a structural neural change. Under these circumstances, the stimuli would have created a 'memory trace' in the short term memory (STM), but would not have been sufficient to create a permanent record in the long term memory (LTM).

This idea of a 'memory trace' is sometimes called an 'engram'. If it is not strengthened or reinforced over time (consolidated) it will fade, much like an old photograph.

Ebbinghaus (1885) was the first researcher to show experimentally that forgetting is a function of time (see Chapter 1, Key study 1, pages 5–6). However, it should be noted that time is not always a 'causal agent' in trace decay. If experiences are not transferred successfully to LTM, trace decay can occur.

More recently, the idea that memories can fade if they are not successfully transferred from STM to LTM has been taken a stage further. Not only is it vital for short term memories to be transferred to long term storage, but also for long term memories to be integrated with existing knowledge. Researchers such as Robert Stickgold (1999) at Harvard Medical School (see RLA 13, page 34) have suggested links between memory consolidation and dreaming. They propose that daily memories need to be incorporated into existing 'neural networks' in order for them to be consolidated, and that is what happens when we dream.

Commentary

A period of dreaming every 24 hours 'restructures' LTM, so that new experiences acquired during the day can be incorporated into existing knowledge. It could be argued that even though information may be in LTM, if it hasn't been successfully incorporated into existing knowledge it will be almost impossible to retrieve.

Memorizing while asleep

Over the years much excitement has been generated about the idea of learning while sleeping. Companies have developed audio tapes to play before you go to sleep, teaching a multitude of things including foreign languages. If Stickgold's suggestion is correct, doesn't it make sense to try to learn while sleeping? In actual fact, Stickgold's findings suggest that sleeping (or more precisely dreaming) helps to consolidate 'daytime experiences', not those occurring during the sleep. This more cynical approach is also shared by other researchers. In his book *Your memory: a user's guide* (1982), Baddeley writes that there is very little evidence that 'sleep-teaching' is effective. He concludes that it is best to be fully conscious when we are attempting to encode new material.

Real Life Application 13:

Memories and dreams

'Scientists have been suggesting links between dreams and memories for two centuries, and many are now convinced that memories from your day become fixed or consolidated as you dream.' Researchers such as Robert Stickgold, at Harvard Medical School, suggest that alternating between deep and light sleep every night is a vital process for the consolidation of new memories. 'While we dream we're busy exploring the links between old and new memories, which may help explain how we can sometimes solve problems in our sleep.'

Carlyle Smith from Trent University in Peterborough, Ontario, proposes that sleep may be especially important for the transfer of memories from short term into long term storage. The area of the brain associated with short term memory, the hippocampus, would easily get overloaded if events were not sent to a much bigger processing area, namely the cortex.

'Even procedural memories like how to ride a bike, which can form without the involvement of the hippocampus, may benefit from the transfer because memory of when and how we learnt that task might help us to supply context, and thus a deeper understanding.' Ironically, because many researchers believe this communication between the hippocampus and cortex is so vital during sleep, any disruption to sleep patterns may well affect the retention of new memories.

'Burning the candle at both ends cheats your brain out of its full night's conversation and makes the whole process futile.' As Stickgold advises: 'You should definitely get your eight hours.'

Article adapted from *New Scientist*, 25 September 1999.

Questions

1 How does dreaming help in the process of consolidating memories?

2 Inhibiting dreaming could induce 'trace decay'. Discuss.

Interference theory

The explanation of interference theory has its roots within psychological literature. It was developed by McGeoch (1932) for the most part as an alternative explanation to the 'Law of disuse', which had been put forward a few years earlier by Thorndike (1913).

Thorndike had suggested that memories naturally deteriorate over time. McGeoch argued that first, this isn't always true and second, it isn't always time that causes memories to be lost. His alternative (the interference theory) argues that what we do between creating our initial memories and recalling them is crucial to the retrieval process. Say we attempt to memorize a theory for a psychology exam, then we try to learn another theory shortly afterwards; if these ideas were similar, we could end up forgetting what we had just learnt.

The theory we had remembered first was interfering with the second. This would be a classic case of pro-active interference (PI). On the other hand, we could find that what we had just learnt was interfering with the first theory. This would be retro-active interference (RI).

Commentary

McGeoch proposed the theory of interference partly as an alternative to the 'Law of disuse'. It suggests that prior or subsequent learning can interfere with the process of recall. However, there are two concerns with this explanation.

1 Interference theory would suggest that we don't actually forget information, it just gets 'hidden' by new or old memories (Govier, 1980).

2 Most of the research into this phenomena has been conducted within the laboratory, using lists of single words or binary associations. Clearly, these methods lack ecological validity; they cannot be generalized to other settings (Postman, 1972).

Summary

- Researchers such as Robert Stickgold have suggested that memories from our day become consolidated as we dream.
- Stickgold proposes that while we dream we're busy exploring links between old and new memories.
- It is also suggested that any disruptions to sleep patterns may well affect the retention of new memories.

Gestalt theory

Gestalt theory is a very specific psychological theory of forgetting. This theory has its roots within an early 'school of thought' in psychology, developed by people such as Wertheimer (1880–1943) and Koffka (1876–1941). Their argument was that we should see the mind as a 'whole', not broken into units. If we want to study a phenomena we should look at it in its completeness, not break it down into simplistic components. If we apply this philosophy to forgetting, we find that memories are 'simplified' or made more 'whole'. There is a tendency for the memory trace to undergo modification in the direction of 'stability' (Koffka, 1935).

Over the years numerous experiments have been conducted in an attempt to illustrate the 'Gestalt philosophy'. A classic study was carried out by Wulf (1922), in which he presented participants with visual material, which they had to recall from memory at later time intervals. What he found was that as the time intervals increased, there was a tendency for participants to 'adapt' the material they were remembering. Two features he identified were described as 'sharpening' and 'levelling' (see Figure 3.1 below).

As can be seen in Figure A, the original drawing was quite smooth. Over a period of a week, participants tended to remember the drawing as much sharper, and therefore reproduced it as such.

Figure B represents the 'levelling' effect. The original drawing was 'over-emphasized' and irregular. After a week, participants tended to remember this drawing as 'less emphasized' and more symmetrical.

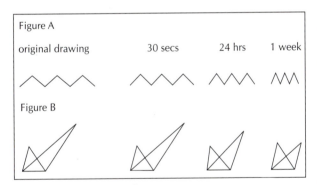

Figure 3.1: Figures A and B.

Wulf concluded that this 'change' in memory over time represented an unconscious move by the participants towards 'order and completeness'. We perceive 'sharp angles' to be more orderly than smoother ones, and we perceive 'subtleness' and symmetry to be more complete.

In Chapter 2 we came across a similar idea under schema theory. Bartlett's (1932) study used a folk story called 'The war of the ghosts'. After an initial reading, people were tested for recall over different time periods. Over time, Bartlett found that people's accounts of the story got shorter and shorter. People made their accounts coherent because they were interpreting the story as a whole. We know stories have a beginning, a middle and an end. People were sacrificing accuracy for 'completeness' – a Gestalt idea.

Commentary

Gestalt theory is useful in explaining why we tend to take 'short cuts' when remembering stories, gossip or rumours. Brunvand (1983) looked at the gossip that was created during the time of the Peter Sutcliff murders (Sutcliffe was the notorious Yorkshire Ripper). What was often found was that stories were generated on the basis of 'old gossip'. They were adapted to fit the current murders.

However, it must be remembered that 'schema theory' could explain this just as well. Also, over the years there have been many studies conducted within this field, but very little empirical evidence has been generated to support Gestalt ideas.

Factors that can influence forgetting

We have looked at some of the main theories, but what about some of the specific factors that can influence forgetting?

Context and 'retrieval cues'

Tulving (1974) proposed that the reason we forget is to do with a lack of relevant cues. He referred to this as 'cue-dependent forgetting'. There are two types of cues:

- context cues, which are external and based around the environment, and
- state dependent cues, which are internal and based on our physiology.

Context cues

The importance of these were illustrated many years ago in a simple study by Abernathy (1940). He found that students remembered more information when they were in familiar surroundings than when they were in unfamiliar ones. Taking witnesses back to the scene of a crime is an example of 'context cueing'.

Flashbulb memory

Under unusual circumstances the location and an event can become synonymous with one another. This is known as 'flashbulb memory'. Some psychologists have suggested that if an event is traumatic or unusual in some way, we are able to associate it within a personal context. For example, one of the classic studies cited in almost every textbook on memory is Brown and Kulik's (1977) study, in which they asked people what they had been doing when they heard that president Kennedy had been assassinated. Nearly 100 per cent could remember, often in great detail. A more recent example would be the death of Diana, Princess of Wales in 1997. Many people can remember where they were and what they were doing when they heard the news of the crash.

Neisser (1982) suggests this sort of finding implies four things.

1 Flashbulb memories are accurate.
2 The memory occurs at the time of the event.
3 Higher levels of surprise and emotionality lead to better memory.
4 Similarities of different flashbulb memories reflect some underlying neural mechanism.

He then goes on to argue that all these implications are dubious. He concludes that the term 'flashbulb' is really misleading.

State dependent cues

In Chapter 2 it was suggested that smells can evoke very powerful memories. This is primarily to do with the location of the olfactory system, but it is also to do with the fact that we have smelt that odour before. The smell is acting as a retrieval cue. Engan and Ross (1973) carried out a study that investigated LTM for smells. Out of the 48 odours that participants had been exposed to 30 days earlier, there was a 67 per cent success rate of correct identification (see Key Study 5).

Chapter 2 also considered the effect of alcohol on memory. It was suggested one of the best ways to retrieve memories encoded while being mildly drunk was to get mildly drunk again. In fact, a study by Goodwin et al (1969) found that alcoholics had difficulty in locating items they had put away when drunk. However, when they were drunk again their location was recalled.

KEY STUDY 5

Researchers:	Engan and Ross (1973)
Aims:	The aim of this study was to illustrate that memory for odours was highly robust over time. This study followed on from an earlier one that had found high levels of recall over short time periods.
Method:	Participants were required to remember 48 odours. Some 30 days later they were exposed to 21 pairs of odours (each pair comprising 1 from the original 48 and 1 new one).
Results:	Correct identification occurred on 67 per cent of occasions.
Conclusions:	Memory for odours is significantly robust over time.

Emotional factors

Over the years there has been much research carried out that investigates the links between emotion and forgetting. In a classic series of studies, participants were hypnotized to feel either happy or sad during the learning of a list of words. Recall was dependent on which emotion they had experienced during encoding. Those who had learnt while feeling sad recalled better while feeling sad, and vice versa (Bower, 1981).

Commentary

Findings such as these illustrate that emotions can act as 'state dependent cues'. As Chapter 4 will show, 'creating the right mood' is very important, particularly in marketing.

Anxiety and depression

We will now consider anxiety and depression, and illustrate their relationship with forgetting.

Anxiety: motivated forgetting

The relationship between forgetting and anxiety has proved to a be a very complex issue. Freud believed that highly traumatic memories were 'banished' to the unconscious, so as to protect us from their effects (a term known as 'repression' or 'motivated forgetting'; see Chapter 1). One of the problems with an idea such as this is setting up a study to illustrate it. Over the years, many of the attempts have focused upon personal recollections.

Waldvogel (1948) found that adult memories of childhood were biased towards recalling pleasant events. Participants could recall 50 per cent pleasant memories, 30 per cent unpleasant and 20 per cent neutral. Waagenaar (1986), conducted a similar study, this time conducting a case study on himself. He kept a detailed personal diary of his life for six years. When he attempted to recall events from this time he found he could recall over half of the positive events, compared to a third of the negative events. This 'rose tinted glasses' effect perhaps underlies the concept of nostalgia. Many of us tend to remember the past selectively.

Commentary

This sort of evidence does suggest that there is a significant tendency for us to 'bias' our recall of past events towards the positive. However, this is not the same as suggesting that we have 'repressed' the negative events.

'Sharpened' memories

Other theorists suggest that moderately emotional events create increases in physiological arousal and this potentially enhances memory recall (Sapolsky, 1998). The problem with assertions such as this is that they nearly all come from experiments using rats learning mazes.

However, McGaugh *et al* (1994) carried out a study which illustrated that moderate arousal can enhance recall in humans (see RLA 14 opposite). Explanations of why moderate arousal creates this enhanced recall become obvious when we consider an evolutionary framework. As Robert Sapolsky very neatly puts it:

'A stressor is a very good time to be at your best in memory retrieval ("How did I get out of this mess last time?") and memory formation ("If I survive this I'd better remember just what I did wrong so I don't get into a mess like this again").'

So there is evidence that anxiety can effect memory in two ways. It can disrupt memory or, alternatively, it can enhance it (see Figure 3.2).

Prolonged anxiety and arousal

Freud's model suggested that when traumatic emotions were placed in the unconscious, they still had the potential to do harm. Over time, repressed

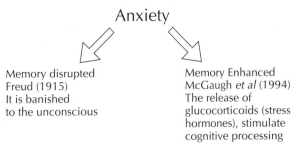

Figure 3.2: Theories regarding anxiety

memories could manifest themselves in neurotic behaviour or physical illness. In this sense they are never truly forgotten.

McGaugh's study considered moderate amounts of stress over a short period of time. However, extreme or prolonged arousal provides the opposite results. We start to forget more. It is suggested that the reason for this is because of prolonged exposure to 'glucocorticoids' (substances released into the bloodstream during stress). Short term exposure is fine; long term exposure damages nerve cells (Sapolsky, 1998).

Real Life Application 14:

Anxiety, depression and forgetting

Material A: 'Sharpening' memory through anxiety

James McGaugh *et al* (1994), at the University of California, published an experiment in *Nature*, suggesting that increased arousal (anxiety) can enhance memory recall. Two groups of participants were read stories. The first group listened to a story about a boy and his mother walking through town; on the way they called into the X-ray department of the local hospital, where the boy's father worked. The second group listened to a very similar story except that the boy was hit by a car and taken to the local hospital X-ray department.

When participants' memories were tested later, the 'stress induced' story created higher memory recall than the 'non-stress induced'. This improvement in memory only applied to the middle part of the story where the trauma occurred. Their memory was no different to the other group in the more mundane parts of the story.

When McGaugh gave the 'traumatic story' group the stress-reducing drug propranolol, he found their memories for the middle (traumatic) part of the story were no better than those in the other group. Because the stress response had been reduced, memory recall lost its 'sharpness'.

Article adapted from *Nature* 371, 702.

Material B: Depression and forgetting

It has long been observed that depressed patients show a variety of cognitive impairments, including lack of concentration and disruptions in STM. However, more recently a new report suggests that depression may cause damage to an area of the brain responsible for the formation of new memories.

Yvette Sheline (1999) and her colleagues at Washington University Missouri found that brain scans using Magnetic Resonance Imaging (MRI) showed that women who suffered from bouts of depression had, on average, a 10 per cent reduction in the size of the hippocampus. (This structure is responsible for the formation of new memories; see Chapter 2.) Sheline believes that the depression caused the damage, and not the other way around.

Article adapted from *New Scientist*, 26 June 1999.

Summary

- McGaugh and colleagues conducted an experiment which suggested that moderate stressors can actually enhance memory.
- They conclude it is the activation of the stress response that causes this enhancement. When the stress response is reduced using propranolol, memory recall is no better than in a control group.
- McGaugh and colleagues propose that this effect has very useful evolutionary benefits. It's a good idea to remember something potentially dangerous, as we can avoid it next time.
- MRI scans have shown that depressed women have, on average, a 10 per cent reduction in size of the hippocampus.
- This structure is located at the base of the brain and is essential for the formation of new memories.
- Sheline believes that depression causes the shrinkage to the hippocampus, and not the other way around.

Questions

1 Summarize, in your own words, how emotional factors such as anxiety and depression can cause forgetting.

2 What are the problems associated with biological explanations of forgetting?

Ageing and forgetting

The issue of memory and old age was considered briefly in Chapter 1. Two studies were cited which implied that severe memory loss is not an inevitability of getting older. While this is true in its extreme form, there is considerable evidence which suggests that varying degrees of memory loss are experienced as we get older.

Methodological issues

Some interesting methodological issues arise through the investigation of ageing and forgetting. Two of these are outlined below.

Who should be used in the study?

Most of the research carried out into ageing and forgetting uses 'cohorts' of elderly individuals who are screened for physical illness (which might be likely to affect memory). One example of a test used is the Anomalous Sentences Repetition Test (Weeks, 1988), which considered indicative of dementia. Once a 'healthy' group has been identified they are usually put through the experiment and compared with 'healthy' younger participants.

Performance in the study

Researchers such as Comfort (1976) suggest that many older individuals get quite distressed when being assessed because they are anxious about failure. A good study, therefore, has to make certain that older participants are not under-performing because of anxiety and low self-esteem.

Problems with 'working memory'

Some studies show deterioration in 'working memory'. Salthouse (1991) found that older adults showed a loss of efficiency when working on mental arithmetic tasks. This could be attributed to an overall decline in cognitive processing in general. In fact, there is evidence that older adults do not use memory strategies as effectively as younger ones. Howe (1988) found that older individuals were less inclined to use existing knowledge to help encode the new material. However, when this idea was pointed out to them they could remember as well as the younger adults.

Recalling the past

It is assumed by many that elderly people are poor at remembering recent events, but good at remembering experiences from the past – particularly the distant past. Grandparents are often heard reminiscing back to when they were children. What has to be remembered when considering memory loss and old age is that forgetting rarely occurs uniformly. Therefore, all these assumptions and stereotypes are not very helpful.

Bahrick *et al* (1975) carried out a study looking at past American high school students. Participants were shown pictures of classmates that were taken 30 years previously in some cases and 50 years previously in others. Recognition was significantly higher for the 30 years than the 50. It appears that ageing reduced recognition.

Being able to 'put a name' to people and common objects appears to be a frequent problem with ageing. Older people report problems with remembering names (Cavanaugh *et al*, 1983).

Helping age-related forgetting

The vast literature of research that has accumulated over the years has allowed psychologists to propose 'normal and abnormal' patterns of ageing and forgetting. When individuals are identified as having problems, various strategies can be implemented.

Yesavage (1983) developed an imagery strategy that could be used by older adults to help them remember people's names. Encouraging older individuals to use diaries, notepads and shopping lists has also proved highly successful (Cavanaugh *et al*, 1983).

Absent-mindedness

A common form of forgetting is often referred to as absent-mindedness. At some time or another, all of us have experienced temporary lapses in memory. Perhaps one of the most common is not being able to remember why you have gone into a room.

Reason (1984) categorizes absent-mindedness in two groups: mistakes and slips. Mistakes are miscalculations in our planning – for example, not taking the correct turning when driving a car. Slips are temporary lapses in memory – for example, not remembering a colleague's name even though you may have worked with that person for years.

Reason (1979) carried out a study in which he asked participants to keep a diary of all occurrences of absent-mindedness. By analysing their experiences he was able to come to a number of conclusions (see Key Study 6). One of the most important conclusions to emerge is the fact that 'memory slips' most frequently occur during highly routine behaviours.

Later, Norman (1981) attempted to put forward an explanation for why absent-mindedness occurs. It is based on 'schema theory'. He suggested that we all develop 'scripts' for everyday actions. If these scripts are used frequently they become habitual. A situation can often 'trigger' a script and once it's running it continues automatically.

I have had the experience of driving to my place of work on a day when it was closed. The realization that it was Sunday only became apparent when I found the gates locked. The journey that I had *intended* to take had begun by using the same roads that I normally take to work. A lapse in concentration and a 'switching over to auto-pilot' (in Norman's model, the 'activation of a schema') resulted in absent-mindedness.

KEY STUDY 6

Researcher:	Reason (1979)
Aims:	Reason was interested in finding out why, when and how absent-mindedness occurs.
Method:	Some 35 volunteers were asked to keep a diary to record all memory lapses and slips during a two-week period. Participants were asked to record these lapses as soon as they realized they had occurred.
Results:	Over the two-week period, the participants jointly experienced 400 memory failures. Reason analysed the data and drew certain conclusions from it.

1 Memory errors were more likely to occur when carrying out habitual tasks.
2 Attempting to carry out an action again, forgetting it had already been completed (these were referred to as storage

failures). Some 40 per cent of the diary entries were errors of this nature.

3 Some participants would start a task and forget to finish it, often switching tasks and beginning something else (these were referred to as test failures). Some 20 per cent of the diary entries were errors of this nature.

4 Participants would carry out a procedure in the wrong order or miss out a stage altogether (these were referred to as subroutine failures). Some 18 per cent of the diary entries were errors of this nature.

5 Program assembly failures occurred when two completely separate procedures were combined together. Some 5 per cent of the diary entries were errors of this nature.

6 Discrimination failures occurred when wrong objects were used to carry out tasks. Some 11 per cent of the diary entries were errors of this nature.

7 Reason was unable to classify the remaining 6 per cent.

Conclusions: Reason was able to produce a detailed account of absent-mindedness, which has allowed other researchers to build on his work.

Individual differences

These have been broken into three categories, each of which is examined below.

Intelligence, personality and forgetting

It might seem reasonable to assume that those individuals with a low IQ score are more likely to forget on tests of memory. Eysenck (1977) surveyed the literature and found no such simplistic relationship. Nevertheless, there is some evidence that people with a 'high' verbal ability or 'spatial' ability (as measured by a standard IQ test), forget less on tests that use these as their stimulus material.

The relationship between personality and forgetting is an interesting one. Eysenck (1977) reviewed the literature and summarized the following points.

1 Extroverts learn quicker than introverts and forget less over short 'retention periods'. When retention periods are increased, extroverts levels of forgetting start to increase.

2 Most of the research comparing introverts and extroverts has focused on the dimension of 'neurotic introversion'. As this is related to generalized anxiety, it could explain why introverts tend to have higher levels of forgetting on memory tests.

Culture differences and forgetting

In his book *Memory observed* (1982), Ulric Neisser devotes a whole section to the study of memory from other cultures. He points out that early explorers and missionaries were often amazed at the astonishing memory abilities of the natives in Africa. Does this mean that Western culture has a higher level of forgetting than many tribal cultures?

The answer appears to be more complex than this. D'Azevedo (1962) studied the 'oral poetry' of the Gola people of West Africa. He found that they place immense importance on their knowledge of the past – what we might call history. 'Forgetting' (in the sense that we understand it) would be insulting to their ancestors and their past culture. Recalling their past helps in shaping their future.

Commentary

Recalling the past is an intrinsic part of the Gola people's culture. Remembering has significance for them because they believe that facts from the past can 'construct' the present. This raises a point that we considered earlier when looking at experiments regarding memory. Getting people to learn meaningless lists of words in an attempt to assess recall is not a very useful exercise. We could argue that even in the West, memory must have significance to us, as it does for the Gola people.

In fact, Mistry and Rogoff (1994) suggest that 'remembering' is a function of the society or culture in which it takes place. We can infer, therefore, that forgetting must be the same. As was pointed out earlier, most research that assesses levels of forgetting is empirical and conducted within a laboratory. When Western and non-Western participants are compared, the latter show higher levels of forgetting. The task they are being asked to undertake has little or no significance for them.

The implications of studying forgetting from a cross-cultural perspective are clear.

1 How much we forget will be related to how important

the information is to us. If it is related to our society or culture it is likely we will remember it.

2 Because of point 1, it is important to remember cultural differences when carrying out experiments that assess levels of forgetting.

Gender differences and forgetting

One of the most controversial areas of forgetting and individual differences concerns gender difference. Studies have shown that women can store (for short periods of time) more random information than men. However, it appears that males can reduce this difference if the random material is organized in some way or is made to have relevance to them (Hutt, 1975). When females are compared with each other, younger women tend to forget names and faces more than older ones (McGuiness, 1976).

Essay questions

1 Describe and evaluate one or more explanation of forgetting in humans (AEB, summer 1999).

2 Why do we forget? (AEB, summer 1989).

3 a What factors and influences have been shown to make humans forget?

b In what ways can these factors and influences be reduced?

Memory and forgetting in the real world

This chapter considers the ways in which memory can be applied to 'real world' settings. It starts by looking at the world of marketing. Next, it examines memory within the context of health and medicine. Then it considers memory within the context of learning and education. Finally, it looks at the ways in which memory research can inform courtroom procedures. Real Life Applications that are considered are:

- RLA 15: Memory and advertising
- RLA 16: Memory and public health scares
- RLA 17: Memories during surgical procedures
- RLA 18: Memories in the doctor's office
- RLA 19: Alzheimer's disease

- RLA 20: Amnesia – a recent case study
- RLA 21: Types of amnesia
- RLA 22: Using mnemonics to study psychology
- RLA 23: The accuracy of eyewitness testimony.

Marketing professionals take memory research very seriously. If a consumer can remember a particular brand or the location of merchandise in a supermarket, they are more likely to make a purchase. But, as we have already seen earlier in this book, memory isn't just a passive 're-run' of a tape. It is reconstructive (Bartlett, 1932). This means that consumers will remember within a context, and use their existing attitudes and beliefs to make their choices. If the marketeer wants to influence consumers' purchasing decisions, they have to 'create a memory' for them.

Memory within the context of marketing

Here there are many things to consider, including an 'interactive targeting' approach, the 'positive association' technique, cue-dependent marketing, the use of 'chunking' in marketing, rehearsal of messages and the order of presentation of messages. Each of these areas in covered in the following text.

The 'interactive targeting' approach

One method that marketing professionals use is the 'interactive' or 'problem-solving' approach. This allows consumers to engage cognitively with the campaign. They will decide which stores, which method of shopping and which products will best meet their needs. By effective market research, a company can target specific products in an attempt to meet these clients' perceived needs.

Television adverts target their audience through time and location slots. Companies buy slots in which the commercial break is sandwiched by programmes whose themes relate to the products. For example, trainers might be advertised during a sporting event, or audio equipment might be advertised during music awards.

Commentary

By allowing a consumer to engage cognitively with the potential product, and then by targeting specific ideas, the marketeer would be making the material more meaningful. Research has shown that meaningful information is learnt more quickly and therefore has a greater chance of being retained (Britt, 1975).

The memory theory related to cognitive engagement and targeting is 'Levels of processing' (Craik and Lockhart, 1972).

The 'positive association' technique

Once consumers have recognized their need for a product or service, they are well on their way to making a purchase. The question is: which brand will they buy? As already mentioned, companies (through market research) attempt to target their products to the most suitable audience. The decision regarding which brand people buy is often based on 'image'. Frequently, consumers will purchase the more expensive product to gain the benefit of a more up-market image.

One way in which products obtain an image is through 'association learning'. We tend to associate brands with certain images. Sometimes companies deliberately make the association images so 'strange' or 'weird', that consumers find it very difficult to understand them. This is a clever technique, as images that are unusual have greater potential for being remembered. Also, there is some evidence that adverts which are perceived to be unique can lead to more favourable assessments by audiences (Meyers-Levy and Tybout, 1989).

Commentary

By associating an existing, well-known, positive image with a product it is highly likely that the product will become more memorable.
The memory theory related to this is 'Imagery' (for example Parkin, 1993).

Cue-dependent marketing

Marketing campaigns need to take into account that consumers will not always be in the same environment when they purchase a product as when they first heard about it. We have already identified that a lack of significant cues could lead to forgetting (see Chapter 3). Clearly, then, if a product is to be remembered there needs to be a consistency to the cues available (Lynch and Srull, 1982). Packaging or a logo can often help here.

Commentary

By re-presenting product cues at a later date, marketeers reduce the chances of forgetting taking place.
The memory theory related to this is 'Cue-dependent forgetting' (Tulving, 1974).

The use of 'chunking' in marketing

If we want to increase the amount of material that we can hold within short term memory (STM) we can arrange it in groups or chunks (see Chapter 1). If marketeers wish to get across complex pieces of information (perhaps containing numbers and so on), they can 'chunk' the material into logical groups. By doing this they can deliver greater amounts of message content in a limited time or space.

Commentary

More information can be processed and retained if it is chunked.
The memory theory related to this is 'Chunking theory' (Miller, 1956).

Rehearsal of messages

If an advert or product slogan allows immediate rehearsal of its material, it is more likely to be retained. Developing a catchy jingle or rhyme can help in this process. We often find ourselves repeating the music or the catch phrase of an advert. The more rhythmical or mesmerizing, the better.

Commentary

Messages that encourage immediate rehearsal of material are more likely to be retained.
The memory theory related to this is 'Working memory' (Cohen et al, 1986). More specifically it relates to the 'articulatory loop'.

Order of the presentation of messages

The order in which material is presented can have effects on what is remembered (see Chapter 1). Glanzer and Cunitz (1966) illustrated the 'serial position effect' – namely, information presented at the beginning of a list (the primacy effect) and at the end of a list (the recency effect) are more likely to be remembered than information presented in the middle. In marketing, this is not only important in terms of how much factual information can be stored, but also the way in which we form 'good' or 'bad' impressions of a product.

Luchins (1964) carried out a study that looked at impression management. In this study, participants each read two versions of the same description of a fictitious person named 'Jim'. In one version, Jim's good attributes were listed first and his not-so-good ones listed last. In the other version, these personal descriptions were reversed.

The study showed that, in the short term what you present first is important (the primacy effect), but after a period of time it is what you presented last that is most important (the recency effect). Clearly 'first impressions count', but in the long term 'last impressions are more important'.

Commentary

The order in which material is presented seems to influence how well it will be retained.
The memory theory related to this is 'Primacy and recency effect' (Glanzer and Cunitz, 1966).

Real Life Application 15:
Memory and advertising

Psychologists advising on the design of advertising campaigns place a lot of emphasis on making adverts more memorable. Outlined below are examples of methods used and of adverts that have used these techniques.

Unique features

By creating a unique feature within the advertisement, companies are making their products or services 'stand out' from the crowd. An advert with a catchy jingle or popular tune uses this technique. From time to time an advertising song finds its way into the charts; this really assists in making it more memorable.

Example of a catchy jingle: 'Shake and vac'

Also, adverts that are weird, strange or unpredictable are employing the unique element.

An example of a 'weird' advert: PlayStation

Immediate rehearsal

Again, catchy jingles fall into this category.

Further examples: 'You can't get better than a Quick Fit fitter'; 'A Mars a day helps you work rest and play'

Chunking

Chunking involves organizing material into 'smaller units' of information. A very good example of this is used in a Lombard Finance advertisement (see below). The company provides loans from £800 to £15,000. It uses these figures within its telephone number. Interestingly, it is utilizing two techniques in one: chunking and mnemonics.

WHAT DO I DO NEXT?

FOR A LOAN FROM
£800 TO £15,000
SIMPLY CALL
0800•2•15000*
AND QUOTE REFERENCE NO. 472 2413

Making adverts more meaningful

This is one of the main reasons advertisers use famous personalities to endorse products. If the audience admires or trusts the celebrity associated with the product, they are more likely to remember it. They are using existing knowledge (or schemas) about the famous person and associating it with the product.

Examples of 'personality endorsement advertising' include: Walkers Crisps, with Gary Linneker and Michael Owen; Barclaycard, with Rowan Atkinson (as a James Bond style agent); and Vodaphone, with Carol Vordemann

Primacy and recency effects

Many companies prefer their television adverts to occupy the first and last 'slots' of a commercial break. Their hope is that the audience is more likely to remember their product or service, because it was the first and last 'ad' before the programme starts again. Also, many direct mail companies 'hide' the price of their products in the middle part of the letter, hoping to minimize its impact.

Examples of companies that use the 'first and last slot' technique include: many car advertisers; Orange Telecommunication.

Summary

- Marketeers take memory theory seriously when considering how to make a campaign more memorable.

- A range of techniques can be used within adverts to make them more memorable. These ideas come from memory research and include the following.

Marketing technique	Memory theory	Name of theorist
Unique features	'Imagery'	(Parkin, 1993)
Immediate rehearsal	'Working memory'	(Cohen *et al*, 1986)
Chunking	'Chunking'	(Miller, 1956)
Adding meaning	'Levels of processing'	(Craik and Lockhart, 1972)
Primacy and recency	'Primacy and recency'	(Glanzer and Cuntz, 1966)

Questions

1 Identify TV advertisements that use the five aforementioned memory theories.

2 What are the advantages and disadvantages in using psychological theory to 'underpin' marketing campaigns?

Memory within the context of health and medicine

Another very important application of memory theory is in the field of health. Like marketeers, health care professionals attempt to convey often complex messages to a wide variety of people. Sometimes the information is general – for example, what constitutes a healthy diet. At other times it's specific – like the key symptoms of meningitis (see extract on page 46, taken from a leaflet about meningitis).

Anxiety and health advice

Health-related information often causes problems of high anxiety. Many people get anxious about things that relate to their health. Research has shown that anxiety directly affects memory recall (see Chapter 3). However, the idea that everyone worries about their health is sometimes overstated.

Often, the reason people don't remember health advice is not because they are over-anxious but because they are not interested. They don't value their health as a priority in their life (Lau *et al*, 1986).

Another reason is 'optimistic bias' (Weinstein, 1987). Many people perceive their risk of developing an illness to be much less than someone else's. It is sometimes referred to as the 'it will never happen to me syndrome'. By adopting this attitude, people feel less threatened (Wills, 1981). It also means there is no point in remembering the health advice, as they do not see themselves at risk.

Commentary

There are two ways in which stress/anxiety can affect memory. First, high anxiety can block out memories and second, it can sharpen memory recall.

The memory theories related to this are 'motivated forgetting' (Freud, 1915) and 'heightened arousal' (McGaugh, 1994).

Real Life Application 16:

Memory and public health scares

During the second half of the 1990s, there was a significant increase in the number of health scares that have been 'unleashed' on the general population of Great Britain (Harris, 1996). People are much more wary about their environment and what they consume. For this reason, it would be logical to assume that people would pay more attention to public information regarding health scares and therefore be good at remembering the facts.

However, research suggests just the opposite. In a very early study, Janis and Feshbach (1953), gave high school students one of three messages designed to promote better dental hygiene: a low, moderate and high fear presentation. They found that the low fear message led to better dental hygiene and argued that the anxiety produced by the moderate or high fear messages triggered a 'defensive avoidance strategy'. This can be seen as an example of Freud's (1915) theory of motivated forgetting (see Chapter 2).

Nevertheless, evidence in this area does not

appear to be clear cut. Reviews of studies within the field (for example Boster and Mongeau, 1984), seem to provide arguments for both sides. More recently, in 1992, Liberman and Chaiken proposed that rather than trying to 'forget' the message (as in motivated forgetting), being personally scared by the contents of a message can actually increase cognitive involvement (which includes memory recall).

Questions

1 Using RLA 16, what are the two ways in which anxiety affects memory recall?

2 Based on Feshbach's (1953) study, how would you design a health campaign to encourage teenagers to eat more fruit?

Summary

- In the last five years there has been a significant increase in the number of public health scares (Harris, 1966).
- Freud's theory of motivated forgetting suggests that people will show a significant reduction in recall of information they find frightening.
- Some researchers (for example, Liberman and Chaiken) propose that in some cases information that people find frightening can be more accurately remembered. This seems to add further evidence to McGaugh's 'heightened arousal' theory (see Chapter 2).

A practical experiment

Examples of two recent health scares include BSE and its link with CJD (1996), and certain brands of oral contraceptive pills and their link with thrombosis (1995). Information regarding these scares often contained technical jargon and was difficult to summarize. You may wish to try an experiment of your own. Read each of the press releases that follow on p. 47, one at a time, then close your book and try to re-write the information. You will be repeating Bartlett's (1932) method. See if you experience results similar to his – for example:

- your reproduction becomes shorter
- you identify the 'gist' of the material but rarely get the exact wording.

Meningitis and Septicaemia

Meningitis is an inflammation of the lining of the brain. It is a rare but very serious illness, though if it's picked up and treated early, most people make a full recovery.

Septicaemia is a form of blood poisoning, which may be caused by the same germs that cause meningitis and often occurs with meningococcal meningitis.

What are the symptoms of meningitis?

Recognising the symptoms could mean the difference between life and death.

Meningitis is not easy to identify at first because the symptoms are similar to those of flu. But it develops quickly, sometimes in just a few hours, and the patient can soon become seriously ill.

The symptoms may not all appear at the same time, and they may be different in young babies, children and adults.

In babies look out for the following:

- a high pitched, moaning cry
- the child being difficult to wake
- refusing to feed or vomiting
- pale or blotchy skin
- red or purple spots that do not fade under pressure – do the 'glass test' (see end of article).

In older children and adults look for the following:

- red or purple spots that do not fade under pressure – do the 'glass test' (see end of article)
- stiffness in the neck – can the person kiss his or her knee, or touch his or her forehead to the knee?
- drowsiness or confusion
- severe headache, vomiting, a temperature
- dislike of bright light.

What are the symptoms of septicaemia?

- a rash, which can be anything from tiny red spots to large blotchy bruises
- skin may be pale and clammy, even though they have a fever
- pain in the limbs or joints

The glass test

Press the side of a glass firmly against the rash – you will be able to see if the rash fades and loses colour under the pressure. If it doesn't change colour, contact your doctor immediately.

Source: The Department of Health. © Crown Copyright 1999.

You can test how much information you have encoded of the above leaflet by reading it for two minutes, then closing the book and trying to recall all the facts.

Figure 4.1

CJD AND CHILDREN – STEPHEN DORRELL STATEMENT

Stephen Dorrell, Secretary of State for Health, today made the following statement to the House of Commons.

' With permission Madam Speaker, I would like to make a further statement about the advice which the Government has received from the Spongiform Encephalopathy. Advisory Committee.

'I begin by reminding the House briefly of the background. The Advisory Committee brings together leading experts in neurology, epidemology and microbiology to provide scientifically based advice on the implications for animal and human health of different forms of spongiform encephalopathy. As I have repeatedly stressed, its members are not Government scientists – they are leading practitioners in their field and it is the function of the Advisory Committee to allow them to pool their expertise to assess the latest scientific evidence that is available.

'Both the Opposition Health Spokesman, and the Leader of the Opposition, stressed last week the importance of reaching decisions on the basis of the scientific evidence. I agree with them. I also agree that it is important that both the evidence on which the Committee reaches its recommendations, and the recommendations themselves, should be made public as soon as practicable. That is why I published the Committee's recommendations last Wednesday and it is why I have today put copies of their latest recommendations, accompanied by a statement from the Chief Medical Officer, in the Vote Office. I can confirm to the House that arrangements are in hand to ensure that the evidence on which these recommendations are based will be published in the scientific journals within the next 4–6 weeks.

'Science is not a substitute for personal or political choice –but it is the only basis on which an informed judgement about these issues can be reached.

'Last Wednesday I informed the House of the Advisory Committee's conclusions about ten new cases of Creutzfeldt-Jakob disease. The statement which the Committee approved at its weekend meeting emphasises that there are only ten cases of this previously unrecognised variant of CJD that have yet been identified, and that the Committee is not in a position to confirm whether or not there is a causal link between BSE and the human disease. The Committee did however repeat its view that the most likely explanation at present of this new form of CJD is that these cases are linked to exposure to BSE before the introduction of the specified offal ban in 1989.

NEW ADVICE ON ORAL CONTRACEPTIVES

Doctors and pharmacists are being informed today of important new information on the combined oral contraceptive pill, which they will be discussing with women using certain brands of the pill.

It is well known that the pill may rarely produce thrombosis (blood clots) involving the veins of the legs. New evidence has become available indicating that the chance of a thrombosis occurring in a vein is increased around two-fold for some types of pill compared with others.

The pills which are more likely to produce a venous thrombosis contain either gestation or desogestrel. Their brand names are as follows:

- Femodene
- Tri-Minulet
- Femodene ED
- Marvelon
- Minulet
- Mercilon
- Triadene.

The Committee on Safety of Medicines (CSM) has therefore issued the following advice.

Women using these pills should continue taking them but should see their doctor, preferably before finishing their current cycle, to discuss whether a change of pill is necessary. Women who cannot visit the surgery, or family planning clinic, before the end of their current cycle should start the next pack.

Users of all other pills do not need to see their doctor or change their pill.

Professor Michael Rawlins, Chairman of the CSM, said today:

' The chance of a woman on the pill experiencing a thrombosis is small. There is no need for anyone to suddenly stop taking the pill. Whatever pill is being taken, the current cycle should be finished. Suddenly stopping the pill could lead to pregnancy and the likelihood of a thrombosis occurring in pregnancy is much higher than on any other pill type.'

Figure 4.2: Press releases from the Department of Health

Also, consider how worrying you personally find the material. The two main theories of anxiety and forgetting suggest you should either recall very little of the material (motivated forgetting – Freud, 1915) or remember quite a lot (heightened arousal – McGaugh, 1994).

Extreme stress

Under certain circumstances, stress can reach extreme levels – for example, while undergoing a surgical procedure. This is very rarely a problem as the patient is fully anaesthetized. However, scientists have recently begun to suggest that this 'physiological high arousal state' could hold the key to why some patients are able to remember events that took place during their operations. Andrade (1999) proposes that the intense adrenaline surge experienced during surgery could be the trigger that allows memories to form.

If we consider these ideas using an evolutionary framework, it appears to make sense. When our ancestors experienced a trauma, the intensity of anxiety they felt allowed the event to become prominent in their memory. This reduced the chances of them making the same mistake again. They learnt (or more precisely remembered) via fear.

Commentary

This sort of research suggests that when someone experiences extreme stress responses, it could trigger memory formation and therefore explain why some people are able to recall events from their operations.
The memory theory related to this is 'heightened arousal' (McGaugh, 1994).

Real Life Applications 17:

Memories during surgical procedures

Researchers at the University of Sheffield believe they have found evidence that patients are able to remember events that took place during a medical procedure while under adequate anaesthesia. It is estimated that three in every thousand patients remember something about their operation when they 'come round', even if it's a trivial remark made by the surgeon.

These findings fly in the face of common sense views about being under an anaesthetic. Typi-

cally, we presume that (due to sedation) new information cannot be retained. Jackie Andrade, one of the researchers, suggests that some aspect of the surgery itself may be responsible for the formation of unconscious memories. She and her colleagues suspect adrenaline to be involved. The surge that is experienced when tissue is damaged during a surgical procedure could be sufficient to trigger memory formation.

Article adapted from *New Scientist*, September, 1999.

Summary

- It is estimated that three in every thousand patients remember something from their operation.
- Contrary to popular belief, anaesthesia does not prevent new memories from being formed. Patients under anaesthesia become aware of their environment from time to time.
- Andrade (1999) believes that an adrenaline surge is responsible for the formation of memories.

Questions

1 In your own words, outline Andrade's findings.

2 Explain how evidence such as this fits in with McGaugh's (1994) heightened arousal theory (see Chapter 2).

Memory and the medical consultation

Another very important application of memory theory is the medical consultation itself. In order for a doctor to ascertain the nature of a patient's problem, the two of them have to engage in a dialogue.

Until recently, medical students underwent very little training in communication skills (Taylor, 1986). Now, however, it features very prominently on all medical degrees. Clearly, if doctors are trained to communicate effectively with their patients, the patients' memories of their meetings will be enhanced.

Studies conducted by Ley in the 1970s suggested that within the consultation patients had good recall of the information they were given first. Also, if the doctor structured (or categorized) the information, the patient's recall was improved. A third finding was that patients who were more familiar with medical terminology remembered more (for a more detailed account see RLA 18 below).

Commentary

Effective communication between doctor and patient during consultations increases the chances that the patient will more accurately recall information discussed.

The memory theories related to Ley's 1970s findings are as follows.

- *Good recall of information given first: 'Primacy effect' (Glanzer and Cunitz, 1966).*
- *Good recall of structured information: 'Hierarchical memory' (Bower et al, 1969)*
- *Good recall if familiar with medical terms: 'Existing knowledge' schema theory (Bartlett, 1932).*

Real Life Applications 18:
Memories in the doctor's office

When people visit a doctor, often they are seeking information and advice. A very common problem that frequently arises during medical consultations is that patients can't remember the information or advice they were given. Anxiety can often interfere with encoding; so, too, can the lack of familiarity with medical terms. Whether the advice is specific or general and its order of presentation can also increase or decrease levels of memory recall.

Ley *et al* (1973), conducted a study looking at how recall of medical information might be improved. He presented two groups of participants with medical statements. One group was told in advance how the statements would be structured; the other group was not. On testing recall, the 'structured' group recalled about 25 per cent more information than the 'unstructured' group. This implies that doctors should, perhaps, explain (before they actually give any information) the way in which they will be giving it – for example:

'First, I'll explain what has caused your problem, then how we are going to treat it. Finally, I'll tell you what you can do to stop your problem coming back.'

One problem with Ley *et al*'s (1973) study, was its lack of ecological validity. It was a classroom-based study, testing people's ability to remember statements from lists. In 1978, Ley conducted another study, this time interviewing patients after a real medical consultation. He compared the doc-

tor's account of the meeting against the patient's recall. On the whole, patients' recall was poor – just over 55 per cent of the information given to them. However, consistent factors appeared to be contributing to the degree of recall.

- Information given first was recalled best.
- No matter how many times the doctors repeated information, it did not significantly improve recall.
- Specific or 'structured' information was remembered better than general information.
- Those who were more familiar with medical terminology remembered more.

These studies prompted Ley and colleagues to produce a handbook, to teach doctors how to communicate more effectively in order to increase memory recall. In follow-up studies, patients whose doctors had read the book recalled, on average, up to 70 per cent more information.

Summary

- Many patients find it difficult to recall the information their doctors give them within the clinical consultation.
- Ley (1973) carried out a study which illustrated that memory recall of information given within the clinical setting could be improved by up to 25 per cent if doctors structured it.
- In 1978, Ley carried out a follow-up study and highlighted a number of areas that doctors could consider when giving information to patients. He produced a booklet of 'good advice'. Doctors who used this in their consultations produced recall rates of 70 per cent more.

Questions

1 Highlight the key features of both of Ley's studies.

2 Identify other 'real life situations' where Ley's findings might be applied.

KEY STUDY 7

Researchers: Ley, Bradshaw, Eaves and Walker (1973).

Aims: The aim of this study was to provide a simple, practical method for increasing recall of information given to patients within the medical consultation. This was done by organizing medical information into labelled categories.

Method: Some 20 undergraduates were given 15 medical statements to read. Some were given the statements in a list format (ordinary condition), others within a categorized format.

List format
1 You have a chest infection
2 and your larynx is slightly inflamed
3 but I think your heart is all right.
4 We will do some heart tests to make sure.
5 We will need to take a blood sample
6 and you will have to have your chest X-rayed.
7 Your cough will disappear in the next two days.
8 You will feel better in a week or so
9 and you will recover completely.
10 We will give you an injection of penicillin
11 and some tablets to take.
12 I'll give you an inhaler to use.
13 You must avoid cold draughts.
14 You must stay indoors in fog
15 and you must take two hours' rest each afternoon.

Categorized format

'I am going to tell you:
• what is wrong with you
• what tests we are going to carry out
• what I think will happen to you
• what treatment you need, and

• what you must do to help yourself.'
'First, what is wrong with you is …' (statements 1-3).
'Second, what tests we are going to carry out are …' (statements 4-6).
'Third, what I think will happen to you is …' (statements 7-9).
'Fourth, the treatment will be …' (statements 10-12).
'Finally, to help yourself you must …' (statements 13-15).

Results: The mean average number of statements recalled in the ordinary condition was 6.5, while the categorized condition was 9.2. This is statistically significant.

Conclusions: The recall for medical information can be increased by the use of explicit categorization.

Loss of memory

Over the last few pages we have been looking at improving memory recall. However, one major area within the medical literature is concerned with forgetting. The term 'amnesia' describes a condition in which people partially or totally lose their memory. There are two classifications of memory loss. First, loss caused by an underlying physical trauma (organic amnesia) and second, loss caused by an emotional trauma (psychogenic amnesia).

Organic amnesia

In the next few pages, we will consider anterograde amnesia, retrograde amnesia and research into amnesia. We will also look at Korsakoff's syndrome (see page 51) and Alzheimer's disease (see page 51) as forms of internal damage, plus surgery-induced memory loss (see page 52) and electro-convulsive therapy (see page 52) as forms of external damage.

Anterograde amnesia

This term describes loss of memory for events and experiences after the physical trauma has occurred. In cases of complete anterograde amnesia the person is unable to form new memories. However, memories formed before the trauma are unaffected.

Retrograde amnesia

This term describes loss of memory for events and experiences prior to the trauma occurring. Because this condition often involves the inability to recall information that was once known, many researchers see this as a retrieval disorder rather than a complete loss of knowledge.

Research into amnesia

There have been numerous case studies of amnesia reported in the scientific literature. Indeed, fiction often uses this as the basis for an exciting 'plot'. Some of you may have seen the romantic comedy film *While you were sleeping*. It tells the story of Peter, a man who awakes from a coma, to find that a complete stranger, Lucy, is claiming to be his fiancée. It was Lucy's dream come true when the man that she fantasized about from a distance was involved in an accident, which left him in a coma. She immediately seized this opportunity to pretend she was part of his life. What makes the story all the more interesting is that when Peter says he has no idea who she is, doctors reassure his family by saying he is suffering from selective amnesia.

Not only is this a classic case of retrograde amnesia, but also it also serves to illustrate how frightening amnesia can be. Imagine waking up to find someone you regard as a complete stranger telling you that you are very close and share memories and experiences together.

Another film that uses amnesia as the focus of the plot is *Overboard* (1987), staring Kurt Russell and Goldie Hawn. Goldie Hawn's character is a wealthy heiress who is rendered amnesic by a tumble from her luxury yacht. In steps Kurt Russell's character who mischievously claims her as his wife. As she is unable to recall anything from her past life, she accepts her new – somewhat poorer – lifestyle.

Fictional stories such as the two examples given are useful because they often give us an emotional insight into conditions. But what of the academic literature? Amnesia, as we mentioned earlier, is divided into physical and psychological causes. Much of the neurological work has focused on physical causes. Again, if you think about it, this category could be divided into two: what we might call internally and externally caused damage. (As mentioned earlier, an example of internal damage is Korsakoff's syndrome. Examples of external damage include surgery induced memory loss and electro-convulsive therapy.)

Korsakoff's syndrome

Korsakoff's syndrome is a form of memory loss caused by excessive alcohol damage. Talland (1965) wrote a classic paper, 'Deranged memory', which was devoted to patients with this condition.

Alzheimer's disease

Other examples of internal damage include the dementures. Probably the best known of these is Alzheimer's disease. Alzheimer's is a progressive, degenerative disease in which 'sticky' substances known as plaques (beta-amyloids) accumulate in the gap between nerve cells. Once there they inhibit cell communication. Memory impairment results when these plaques build up in areas of the brain heavily involved in memory (such as the hippocampus).

The reason these plaques occur is that the substance that leads to the production of amyloids (Amyloid Precursor Protein – APP) goes wrong. It is believed that amyloids are normally involved in the production of long term memories (Bliss and Rose, 1997). Clearly, if scientists could develop a drug that prevents APP from going wrong, they would be well on their way to creating a cure for Alzheimer's.

Real Life Applications 19:

Alzheimer's disease

Dame Iris Murdoch, one of the greatest writers of the 20th century, suffered from a neuro-degenerative disease, very likely Alzheimer's. Like many patients with presumed Alzheimer's, Dame Iris had much more difficulty with learning and remembering current events than with retrieving long-established semantic memories. Her expressive vocabulary became reduced to a fraction of its former glory. She could not name many common objects and was severely impaired at naming people. Patterson and Hodges tested Dame Iris on their category fluency tests in which normal people in their 60s and 70s produce an average of eighteen animal names and sixteen bird names. She only managed three animal names and no birds. They sadly predicted that her latest book, *Jackson's dilemma* (1993-94) would be her last.

Adapted from 'When memory loses its meaning', by Patterson and Hodges, *MRC News*, summer 1997.

(Iris Murdoch died in 1999.)

Summary

- Dame Iris Murdock, the famous novelist, was diagnosed as suffering from Alzheimer's disease.
- She had more difficulty in remembering current memories than long term semantic memories.
- Patterson and Hodges found that on their category fluency tests, Murdoch could only identify three animals and no bird names. Normal 60- or 70-year-olds remember, on average, eighteen animals and sixteen birds.

Questions

1 In your own words, briefly explain what is believed to cause Alzheimer's disease.

2 Why are diseases such as Alzheimer's used by scientists to explain 'normal' memory functioning?

Surgery induced memory loss

An example of external damage would be brain surgery. One of the most classic case studies of 'surgically induced amnesia' was that of HM (Milner *et al*, 1978). He underwent surgery to correct a serious epileptic seizure condition and had the hippocampus removed. His surgery successfully cured the epilepsy. However, HM permanently lost the ability to learn new things. He could only name friends and recall stories that related to them if he had known them prior to surgery.

[N]ew events, faces, phone numbers, places now settle in his mind for just a few seconds or minutes, before they slip like water through a sieve (Blakemore, 1988).

HM is very good at developing trick associations to help him remember things. But the trouble is that it works only so long as he can keep repeating it to himself. As soon as he is distracted he forgets the whole thing. It never gets stored in long term permanent memory (Ornstein and Thompson, 1985).

Commentary

HM suffered from anterograde amnesia. His short term memory (STM) was fine. However, it could not be transferred to long term storage (LTM). It could be argued, though, that HM *could* transfer information to LTM;

what he *couldn't* do was retrieve. Scientists are still unsure as to which explanation is correct for anterograde amnesia.

The memory theory that can be applied here is the 'multi-store model' (Atkinson and Shiffrin, 1968, 1971).

HM showed successive improvements on motor tasks without having any awareness that he had undertaken these tasks before (see information on procedural memory in Chapter 1).

Another example of this comes from anecdotal archive evidence. Claparede (1911) greeted an amnesic patient by shaking hands while holding a pin. The next day the patient had no recollection of the event, but was very reluctant to shake hands again.

Commentary

Studies such as those on HM and by Claparede illustrate that amnesia is far more complex than just total memory loss. In both of the above cases procedural memory (memory for 'doing' things) was clearly still intact.

Electro-convulsive therapy (ECT) and memory loss

Another external cause of damage that often results in amnesia is electro-convulsive therapy (ECT). This highly controversial shock treatment is used primarily in severe cases of depression. It involves applying a moderate electric current to the head, which results in a controlled seizure. Often, patients lose memories of events just prior to the treatment. Indeed, Carl Duncan (1949) found this to be true of rats who were given ECT.

Squire and Cohen (1982) conducted a questionnaire on patients who had undergone ECT. The patients were asked if they recognized the titles of television programmes from 1957–72. What the questionnaire established was that the more recent titles were poorly recalled, whereas older titles were recalled much better. It appears ECT creates a form of retrograde amnesia by interfering with memory consolidation.

Commentary

ECT can affect the way in which memories are transferred to LTM.

The memory theory which relates to this is 'consolidation theory' (Hebb, 1949).

Real Life Applications 20:
Amnesia – a recent case study

Ex-Channel Four news presenter Sheena McDonald revealed yesterday that she was finding it hard to get work after a road traffic accident which left her in a coma for three days. Her partner Alan Little, BBC Moscow correspondent, said: 'The thing about memory loss is you don't know what you've forgotten. So it's not frightening until it starts to resolve itself. Then when it starts to come back you start to think what else has gone?' Sheena could not remember events prior to her accident.

Article adapted from *The Daily Record*,
Monday 13 September 1999.

Summary

- Often, the day-to-day emotional effects of amnesia are understated within academic research.
- The most frightening thing about amnesia is that you don't know what you have forgotten until it resurfaces again.

Questions

1 Identify some of the emotional feelings amnesic patients may experience.

2 Having read RLA 20, what type of amnesia was Sheena McDonald suffering from?

Psychogenic amnesia

The second type of amnesia, psychogenic amnesia, nearly always follows some unpleasant and emotionally disturbing event, and the degree of impairment can vary (Parkin, 1987). The two major categories of this are 'hysterical' and 'fugue' amnesia.

Hysterical amnesia

Janet (1904), wrote detailed accounts of hysterical amnesia in which victims lost total memory of the events leading up to bad news. Interestingly, nearly all accounts of hysterical amnesia are of the retrograde variety.

Fugue amnesia

Fugue amnesia has an even more bizarre presentation. It has been defined as:

'the sudden onset of wondering with clouding of consciousness and a more or less complete amnesia for the event' (Berrington *et al*, 1956).

Explanations

The French psychiatrist Pierre Janet (1904) proposed an explanation for both types of psychogenic amnesia. Her suggestion was that under normal circumstances our autobiographical memories are held together by a strong sense of personal identity. She argued that the strength of our personal identity is genetically determined. Individuals with 'weak energy' for their personal identity were more likely to suffer from psychogenic amnesia.

Probably one of the most influential theories was proposed by Freud (1914). He suggested that psychogenic amnesia was a defence reaction to painful earlier experiences.

A more recent explanation has been put forward by Schacter *et al* (1982). What is interesting about this is that it combines parts of each of the two other explanations. It suggests that our episodic memories are unique because they relate to us personally. If through some sort of repression our episodic memories become separated from our perception of personal identity, then we cannot put these personal episodic memories into context. In a milder form this becomes 'hysterical' amnesia; in a severe form it becomes fugue.

Commentary

Hysterical and fugue amnesia are complex disorders, which combine concepts relating to our personal identity, our personal episodic memories and 'repression' (motivated forgetting).

The memory theories related to this are 'motivated forgetting' (Freud, 1915) and 'Schema theory: a mental framework of how we remember ourselves and others' (Bartlett, 1932).

Real Life Applications 21:
Types of amnesia

Material A: Hysterical amnesia

Loss of memory without an underlying physical cause is referred to as psychogenic amnesia. One form of this disorder is known as 'hysterical' amnesia. This is diagnosed when a person experiences sudden memory loss following a traumatic event. The individual cannot recall memories from that period. Grinker and Spiegal (1945) used the barbiturate drug sodium pentothal to elicit combat experiences of soldiers during World War Two. They found this drug reduced anxiety, therefore allowing the men to recall painful memories, which were too difficult to access under normal states of consciousness. This sort of case study raises questions about the nature of hysterical amnesia. For example, have memories of painful experiences really been 'locked away', or is the patient under normal circumstances just not willing to disclose memories they find highly disturbing?

Adapted from the book *Men under stress* by Grinker and Spiegal, 1945.

Material B: Fugue amnesia

Another form of psychogenic amnesia is referred to as 'fugue' amnesia. The term is taken from the French word '*fugerer*', meaning to run away. The individual suffering from this disorder is often found wandering far from home in a confused state with a lack of knowledge of their past history. In a Freudian sense, the 'running away' component of fugue can be seen as symbolic of trying to escape from memories that are too painful to deal with in a conscious sense. It is a defence reaction.

Material C: Psychogenic amnesia and the law

Both hysterical amnesia and fugue states have serious implications for legal trials. If a defendant was suffering from either of these disorders while carrying out a crime, to what extent can they be held liable for their actions? The term 'automatism' is used in law to describe any act performed automatically – that is, without any conscious thought or reflection. Clearly, being amnesic during the crime would imply that the defendant would have no recollection or awareness of what they were doing.

In a case in 1959, a defendant named Podola, who was being indicted for capital murder, raised a preliminary issue that he was unfit to plead owing to loss of memory of events prior to and including the alleged homicide. The jury found that Podola was not suffering from a 'genuine memory loss', and he was found guilty of capital murder.

Case study adapted from R v Podola (1959), 3 All ER 418, Court of Criminal Appeal.

Summary

- Hysterical amnesia is diagnosed when a person experiences sudden memory loss, following a traumatic event.

- Grinker and Spiegal studied 'battle stressed' soldiers. They found that by using the drug sodium pentothal, battle memories that had been forgotten were resurrected.
- Fugue amnesia is taken from the French word 'fugere', meaning to run away. It describes a condition in which the person is found wandering in a confused state with memory loss.
- The law states that a person suffering from amnesia is 'unfit to plead'. However, as in the case of R v Podola (1959), this is a very difficult case to prove.

Questions

1 In your own words describe the two types of psychogenic amnesia.

2 Briefly evaluate the explanations for psychogenic amnesia.

Memory, learning and education

Another major area, and possibly the most obvious, where memory can be applied, is within the field of learning and education. Whether we are learning how to ride a bike for the first time or learning new and complex theories for our A levels, we need to retain new information. As we have been illustrating throughout this book, recall is dependent on personal experiences and context. For this reason, those involved in designing educational programmes pay great attention to how information is learnt.

Rote learning

This is the name given to the process of memorizing something by simply repeating it over and over again. An important aspect of rote memory is that it is learning for learning's sake. Reber (1985) defines it as being 'devoid of meaningfulness'. Students memorize facts to help them pass exams. You may have been unfortunate enough to have a teacher at school who used to say things like: 'You don't need to know why, just remember it.' Clearly this will hinder the learning process.

A meaningful context for learning

We have already discussed Craik and Lockhart's (1972) 'levels of processing model' (see Chapter 2). This suggested that the more meaningful material could be made, the more deeply it would be processed. Good teachers should therefore provide their students with a meaningful context in which to learn. How can this be done? Below we will take a look at three different ways: using examples, through organization and through environment.

Using examples
One method of meaningful context might involve giving students stimulating and personally relevant examples. We all like to be told a good story, and if knowledge can be imparted through the vehicle of story-telling it helps to place the information within a context.

Commentary
Using examples is based upon Bartlett's (1932) schema theory. By making information relevant to the learner, you are using existing knowledge, thereby increasing memorability. It must be remembered, however, that examples should be suitable and relevant to the audience listening.

Organization
I am sure everyone of us at some time has experienced the problems associated with being disorganized. Much research has focused on the benefits of organizing material prior to learning (for example, Collins and Quillian's 1969 'network' model; see Chapter 2).

Additionally, as discussed earlier in this chapter, Ley and colleagues (1973) illustrated that patients' memories for medical information could be improved by explaining to them how subsequent information was going to be given. This idea should also be used within education. Good teachers should start lessons with an outline of what they will be covering.

However, organization can also occur at the end of learning. Nearly all learning materials will provide summaries at the end of sections. This is to help readers to simplify all the material they have just read. It also acts as a guide to highlight the important points. Reder and Anderson (1980) found that a group of students who learnt from summaries remembered more material than a group who learnt from the complete text.

Commentary
Organizing material improves memory recall. Studies such as Ley *et al*'s (1973) illustrate that informing people how material will be presented improves memory recall. Teachers can outline lessons and describe their objectives before delivering the material. Students will therefore know what topics will be covered and in what order.

Environment
We have already looked at factors that can influence forgetting (see Chapter 3). One of these was lack of 'context cues'. If we learn within a particular environment, we will recall best within a very similar setting. This is one reason why, if students are preparing for examinations, they need to learn in an environment that is similar to the one they will be recalling in. You won't be able to revise in the main hall where the exams will be held. However, certain things can be controlled. As Child (1973) points out, there are many distractions that can affect encoding:

'*A noisy classroom, TV or radio in the background at home, roadworks or building noises, or even the voices of others constitute a distraction for most people.*'

Memory aids
All students at some stage of their careers have used memory aids in one form or another. In RLA 5 (see page 12) we looked at the oldest of these 'aids' – that is, mnemonics. If you recall, it involves linking or associating rhymes or other memorable devices to whatever it is you wish to remember.

Commentary
Mnemonics are a useful technique to help you recall factual information. By making up a rhyme that incorporates the first letters of the material you are trying to remember, you are increasing memorability by association. The more bizarre or rude our images, the more likely we are to remember them (Anderson, 1995). RLA 22 (below) looks at how mnemonics can be used to learn information from this book.

Real Life Application 22:

Using mnemonics to study psychology

Let us assume that you are preparing for a psychology exam. The topic that you are looking at today is 'Theories of forgetting'. You want to create a summary sheet based on the researchers' names mentioned in Chapter 3. This can then be used as the basis of your revision. Below is an example of part of a list of researchers incorporating some mnemonics, just to illustrate how it might work.

TRACE DECAY
Hebb	H = Hello
Stickgold	S = Sexy

INTERFERENCE
Thorndike	T = This
McGeoch	M = Makes
Govier	G = Good
Postman	P = Psychology

GESTALT
Wertheimer	W = Women
Koffka	K = Know
Wulf	W = What's
Brunvand	B = Best

We have now created three 'sayings'. The next process would be to learn the sayings and associate the researchers' names with words in the saying. This is often best achieved through repetition. Once you have remembered the names, the final stage of the process has to begin. The researchers need to be associated with their contributions (what they did or said). This can be achieved by creating bizarre images and associations between their names and their work. Take a look at the following examples.

- Stickgold (99): we could have had a DREAM about a GOLD STICK last year (1999).
- Brunvand (83): BRUN sounds like BROWN; VAND sounds like van. Someone could be gossiping about a brown van in the Yorkshire Dales. This was where the 'Yorkshire ripper' carried out his murderers.
- Postman (72): The POSTMAN is bringing us two warning letters. First warning about 'ecological validity'. Second warning about not 'generalizing' our findings to other settings.

Summary

- Mnemonics are a very useful method for helping to remember lists of items.
- Because psychology exams require you to remember the names and dates (if possible) of researchers who carried out studies, we can use the mnemonic method to help.
- Through repetition we learn to associate our saying's initial with the name of the researcher.
- Finally, through creating bizarre images we can relate the name of our researcher with their findings.

Question

1 Try this technique for yourself, and see how well it works for you!

Memory within the context of the court room

We have already seen that many academics (for example Graham Davies, 1994) believe that eyewitness testimony is not reliable and therefore should not be used in courts (see Chapter 2, RLA 8 on page 22). In fact, in 1980, Buckhout showed a short film of a mugging on prime time television, and then asked viewers to phone in and identify the assailant. Over 2,000 people responded, but only 14 per cent were able to make a correct identification. Clearly this was not a controlled experiment, but it does highlight the high levels of inaccuracy found within this area.

Reconstructive memory revisited

Bartlett (1932) was the first researcher to propose that human memory is not like a camera (see Chapter 2). We don't record information literally. If this was the case then virtually 100 per cent of viewers would have made a correct identification in Buckhout's study above. Again, as seen in RLA 8, studies show that we 'reconstruct' memory using our existing knowledge, and that includes stereotypes. Bull and Rumsey (1988), found that people are happy to make a conviction on appearance alone – that somehow we know what a criminal looks like. It seems that elderly people are more prone to this than younger people (Yarmey, 1983).

The notion that we reconstruct memories in the present has been taken further by Elizabeth Loftus. In many studies, she and her colleagues have shown that if a witness is exposed to new information between seeing an event and recalling it, this can have profound effects on the subsequent recall. However, not all researchers agree with this. McCloskey and Zaragoza (1985) argue that new information between encoding and recall can bias the way people may respond to questioning, but it doesn't change the original memory itself. It is for this reason that some believe hypnosis is a good method of retrieval. Potentially it can circumnavigate the dangers of 'leading questions', by subconsciously activating the memory.

Misleading information

Loftus (1975) conducted a study that looked at giving misleading information. She presented a film of a road traffic accident and, after showing it, asked one group to estimate how fast they thought the car was going when it passed the 'yield' (giveway) sign. The second (experimental) group were asked the same question, but they were given false information. They were asked to estimate the speed when the car passed the barn. Of course, there was no barn.

Interestingly, 17 per cent within this condition thought they remembered a barn, compared to 3 per cent in the first group. Clearly, the suggestion of a barn had been enough for some participants to incorporate it into their recall.

Commentary

Memory is a dynamic process. We can incorporate information we receive after witnessing an event, and believe that it was present at the time. However, we must be cautious of studies such as these. They attempt to be as naturalistic as they can, but in real life we don't sit watching a film of an event, we are usually interacting with the event itself (Stephenson, 1988).
The memory theory that relates to this is 'Schema theory' (Bartlett, 1932).

KEY STUDY 8

Researcher:	Loftus (1975)
Aims:	This experiment tested the idea of 'schema theory'. It proposed that participants' memories of an event could be 'falsified' if they were given misleading information after witnessing an event.
Method:	The participants viewed a film showing a car accident. After this they were asked to fill out a questionnaire consisting of questions relating to the film. One group was asked questions about events that actually happened; the other group was asked questions that included events that had not occurred. One such question asked the participants how fast the car was going when it passed the barn. There had been no barn shown on the film. A week later, participants were questioned regarding their memory of the accident.
Results:	With the question about the barn, 17.3 per cent believed they had seen a barn (in the false information group) compared to 2.7 per cent in the genuine group.
Conclusions:	By introducing false information, participants were made to believe they had seen something when, in fact, they hadn't.

Memory of a real life event

Later, Loftus and Greene (1980) tested memory for a 'real life' staged event, rather than a film. A man (who did not have a moustache) entered a classroom, picked up a book and started an argument with the lecturer. Later, the students were asked about their observations of the man. In one condition they were asked: 'Did the man who was tall and had a moustache say anything?' In another, they were asked: 'Was the moustache light or dark brown?'

Those students who were exposed to the first condition were more misled (by thinking he had a moustache) than those in the second condition. Clearly, if you want to mislead someone, it pays to be more subtle.

Leading questions

During court cases, barristers are able to cross examine witnesses. Clearly, the more skilled the barrister, the more likely they will be to 'lead the witness'. Usually this provokes an 'objection' response from the second barrister that their witness is being manipulated. However, sometimes the manipulation can be so subtle that it goes unnoticed, but its effect is substantial (see RLA 23).

Real Life Application 23:

The accuracy of eyewitness testimony

Loftus (1979) has shown that the way in which people are asked questions can affect their responses. In a study participants were shown a film of a car accident and asked to fill out a questionnaire.

They were divided into two groups. One group was asked the question: 'About how fast were the cars going when they hit each other?' The other group was asked: 'About how fast were the cars going when they smashed into each other?'

Interestingly, the group that had read the word 'smashed' rated the speed of the impact to be significantly higher than the group who had read the word 'hit'. Clearly, the subtle difference between the words had prompted differences in recall.

A week later, the participants were re-interviewed and asked: 'Did you see any broken glass?' The fact was, there had been no broken glass on the film. Despite that, 32 per cent of participants who had originally read the word 'smashed' believed they had seen glass on the film, compared to 14 per cent who had originally read the word 'hit'. Once again, the choice of words affected the retrieval process.

Summary

- Loftus has shown that the wording used to illicit memories has a significant effect on memory recall.
- Participants are prone to distortions of recall based upon the choice of words used to prompt recall.
- Barristers use this to their advantage, by 'priming' witnesses in the choice of words they use.

Questions

1 Summarize the key points of Loftus's study.

2 What are the problems of conducting a study such as this in the laboratory?

3 What does research such as this tell you about the process of retrieval? (A tip: think about schema theory.)

Essay questions

1 a Outline two applications of research into memory.

  b Outline and evaluate research findings on which these applications are based (AEB, January 1999).

2 In what ways can memory theory be applied to real life settings?

3 In what ways can marketeers use memory theory to improve retention of adverts?

4 In what ways can teachers/health educators use memory theory to improve retention of information?

5 How can the psychology of memory be applied to the law?

Theory cross-reference section for Chapter 4

Because this chapter considers real life uses of memory, it is felt that a theory cross-reference section would be useful to the reader. All of the theories referred to have been discussed earlier in this book. The list on the following page gives a summary of the theory, the name of the researcher associated with it and a page number where more details can be found. As you have probably now read Chapter 4 you will recall that the commentary sections within this chapter also identify the theories listed below. However, they provide more information by explaining exactly how they apply to the real life applications.

Application	Theory and researcher(s)
MARKETING	
Interactive targeting: creating meaning for the audience	'Levels of processing' Craik and Lockhart, 1972) Page 42
Positive association: unique features	'Imagery' (Parkin, 1993) Page 43
Cue-dependent marketing	'Cue-dependent forgetting' (Tulving, 1974) Page 43
Chunking	'Chunking theory' (Miller, 1956) Page 43
Rehearsal of messages	'Working memory' (Articulatory loop) (Cohen et al, 1986) Page 43
Messages at the beginning and end	'Primacy and recency' (Glanzer and Cunitz, 1966) Page 43
HEALTH AND MEDICINE	
Anxiety and fear	'Motivated forgetting' (Freud, 1915) 'Heightened arousal'

Application	Theory and researcher(s)
	(McGaugh, 1994) Page 45
Good recall of information given first in medical consultation	'Primacy effect' (Glanzer and Cunitz, in 1966) Page 49
Good recall of structured formation given in medical consultation	Hierarchical organizintion' (Bower et al, 1969) Page 49
Good recall if familiar with medical terms within medical consultation	'Schema theory' (Bartlett, 1932) Page 49
Anterograde amnesia	'Multi-store model' (Atkinson and Shiffrin 1968, 1971) Page 50
ECT-induced amnesia	'Consolidation theory' (Hebb, 1949) Page 52
Psychogenic amnesia	'Motivated forgetting' (Freud, 1915) Page 53 'Schema theory' (Bartlett, 1932) Page 53
LEARNING AND EDUCATION	
Using examples within teaching	'Schema theory' (Bartlett, 1932) Page 55
Organizing material within teaching	'Hierarchical organization' (Bower et al, 1969) Page 55
Memory aids	'Mnemonics' (Buzan, 1974) Page 55 'Images' (Anderson, 1995) Page 55
COURT ROOM	
Reconstructing events (eye witness testimony)	'Schema theory' (Bartlett, 1932) Page 56

# Advice on answering essay questions

Chapter 1

1 This is asking you to identify various approaches to the study of memory, then analyse the strengths and weaknesses of these approaches. You could look at the highly structured experimental tradition of Ebbinghaus and compare this to the more 'dynamic' and real life approach of Bartlett. You may wish to include Freud as an example of a theory that stands alone.

2 This question is asking you to look at historical figures in the development of memory research and identify exactly what their contribution was. Then it asks you to assess to what extent there was cohesion and progression within the theories. You could suggest that many researchers identified a short/long term split (even though they called it different things). However, because they focused on different aspects of memory, their methods varied.

3a You are being asked to identify a general concept in memory. This could include STM/LTM, retrieval (including techniques – for example, mnemonics), metamemory or photographic memory.

3b This part is asking you to assess your chosen concept. You need to look at the limitations of the concept, how applicable it may be to real life settings and consider criticisms.

Chapter 2

1 This question requires you to identify one theory, and assess its strengths and weaknesses. You could consider the methods it was based on, how applicable it is to real life, how generalizable it is and look at opposing theories.

2 This question is specifically asking you to focus on the effects of organizing material on memory. You need to identify the work of Collins and Quillian (1969) and Bower *et al* (1969). You also need to make an assessment of how organization takes place and why it helps facilitate memory.

You could justifiably mention points related to imagery, but don't make this the focus of your essay, as organization is broader than just imagery.

3a You are required to highlight the key features of schema theory. These could include the following:

- We construct memory from existing knowledge.
- Memory is dynamic.
- Memory is not a literal recording of events.
- Expectations can influence how we remember.

Obviously, you would need to elaborate on these points.

3b In this part of the question you are asked to assess how useful schema theory is in real life. You can cite 'mistaken identity' research and also talk about 'stereotypes' and 'expert knowledge' as examples of existing knowledge.

Chapter 3

1 In this question you are given a choice of considering one or more theories. If you choose one you need to be prepared to look at it in some depth. If you choose a number it is possible to compare them with one another. You need to think about the evidence that backs up these theory (theories) and also how they may be applied to real life settings.

2 This question is asking you to provide a whole range of evidence. You need to assess the theories in much the same way as Question 1. It may be a good idea to conclude this essay by way of a summary. An example would be: 'Humans forget for a variety of reasons.'

3a Rather than just focusing on theories, this question is asking you to identify a range of influences that make us forget. Your answer would need to include things such 'state dependent cues', motivated forgetting and so on.

3b This part of the question is asking you to analyse the factors you have identified in Part 3a, and give suggestions as to how they might be reduced. You might suggest that learning in a similar environment to the one in which you are going to retrieve has been shown to help.

Chapter 4

1a Here you can choose two areas we have looked at in Chapter 4. You may wish to look at marketing, health and medicine, education and learning or the court room.

1b First, you need to discuss research that has been carried out in these areas. Then you need to critically evaluate this work, asking questions such as: 'Was the research carried out in the natural environment or a lab?'

2 This question is very general. A good answer would give a wide range of real life applications. You would need to discuss the research on which these applications are based and give a critique.

3 This question is specifically asking you to take your evidence from the field of marketing, and in particular advertisements. You need to select relevant studies and ideas, then critically assess them. You need to show how theory can improve the memorability of material within an advertising setting.

4 This is an identical question to 3, except the chosen topic is education and learning. It needs to be answered in the same way as 3.

5 This is an identical question to 3 and 4, which should be answered in the same way as outlined for 3.

A Advice on answering short answer questions

Chapter 1

RLA 1

1 Foetuses have little control over what experiences they are exposed to 'in utero'.

  You could give more evidence for the Freudian concept of childhood amnesia – we can't remember our womb experiences or our birth!

2 An advantage could be that it's a well-controlled study.

A disadvantage could be that it's a very small sample (16).

RLA 2

1 Jung carried out no scientific studies to verify his claims; they were all based on case studies and his interpretations.

2 Recovering 'primitive memories' could be useful to individuals who lack confidence or have poor self-esteem; they can experience behaviours that are natural and spontaneous. Recalling these memories could be potentially harmful if the therapist does not prepare a safe and 'emotionally unjudging' environment.

RLA 3

1 You must summarize using your own words.

2 It is when clients/patients (usually while undergoing therapy) start to believe they were abused as children. There is no evidence for this being true.

RLA 4

1 You must summarize using your own words.

2 Because human brains communicate using a network of nerves, it means all pathways interconnect with one another. This allows a 'richness' of information. PDP within machines attempts to mimic this concept.

RLA 5

1 You must summarize using your own words.

2 It allows people to 'attach' existing knowledge to a new concept (the material they wish to learn), and this acts as a 'trigger' in the retrieval process. By accessing the existing knowledge they also retrieve the new information.

RLA 6

1 You must summarize using your own words.

2 If humans can make accurate assessments of whether they possess some information or not, this could be helpful in determining whether a situation requires caution (this would be an evolutionary explanation).

RLA 7

1 Sperling (1960) found that participants could hold in their memories very detailed images but only for very short periods of time (less than half a second). Eidetic imagery appears to be a similar ability, but people are able to hold images for much longer.

2 One reason could be that left hemisphere behaviours (such as verbal and numerical abilities) are not as developed in children – implying children are capable of using more right hemisphere behaviours (such as imagination and imagery).

Chapter 2

RLA 8

1 Existing knowledge can include attitudes, beliefs and stereotypes. These biases will shape the way in which new information is encoded and retrieved.

2 Use examples from eyewitness identification to illustrate how images (such as the one portrayed by Ellis – see Material C) influence encoding and retrieval.

RLA 9

1 Organization of material prior to learning allows individuals to integrate and relate the new material to what is already known. Using categories or headings is an excellent example of this.

2 The lack of 'ecological validity' is a flaw. Word units are rarely experienced in real world memory. We must question, therefore, how far results from this type of study can be generalized to other areas.

RLA 10

1 This could help people who have experienced memory loss through accident or illness. It could help scientists to understand the bio-chemical nature of memory better.

2 There could be ethical problems – for example, who should have access to nootropics. Do they actually work? (See comments by Kerr, 1997.)

RLA 11

1 You must summarize using your own words.

2 An advantage could be that 'biologically based' interventions could be developed for memory problems. A disadvantage could be that the biological perspective is 'reductionist'.

RLA 12

1 We must be careful that we do not assume a causal link. It is more likely that there is an intervening variable at work, namely physical health overall. The relationship perhaps looks like this.

2 Two studies that suggest memory loss is not inevitable are Harris and Sunderland (1981) and Rabbitt (1994). Two studies that suggest ageing does lead to memory loss could include Salthouse (1991) and Bahrick et al (1975).

Chapter 3

RLA 13

1 Stickgold (1999) suggests that dreaming allows memories that have passed from STM to LTM during the day, to be 'incorporated' into existing memories.

2 Because of what was outlined in Question 1, inhibiting dreaming could prevent 'incorporation' and therefore new memories would be lost (trace decay).

RLA 14

1 You must summarize using your own words.

2 Biological explanations are reductionist. Also they tend to use animals as their participants.

Chapter 4

RLA 15

1 Identify current TV commercials.

2 An advantage is that using psychological theory improves the memorability of material. A disadvantage could be that by applying psychological theory we may reduce creativity. By applying theory you may find you can't present material in such an artistic way.

RLA 16

1 It can repress memory through motivated forgetting (Freud, 1915). It can enhance memory through heightened arousal (McGaugh, 1994).

2 Feshbach (1953) found the low fear message led to better dental hygiene. You need to adopt this principle in encouraging teenagers to eat more fruit. Be as imaginative as you can.

RLA 17

1 You must summarize using your own words.

2 McGaugh (1994) suggests that it makes evolutionary sense to encode events while experiencing anxiety, so this information can be used in future avoidance strategies. It follows therefore that patients are able to encode while undergoing surgery – a time of extreme heightened arousal.

RLA 18

1 You must summarize using your own words.

2 Use any situation similar to a medical consultation where anxiety is potentially high – for example going to the dentist or solicitor, being in court and so on. (Be as imaginative as you can.)

RLA 19

1 Using the information provided in the text, summarize in your own words.

2 The medical approach often studies disorders to identify what has gone wrong with a process. By comparing a person with a disorder to a 'healthy' individual, scientists are able to pin-point what underlies normal functioning.

RLA 20

1 You could mention disorientation, depression, anxiety, fright and so on.

2 Retrograde amnesia.

RLA 21

1 You must summarize using your own words.

2 Janet (1904) suggested that psychogenic amnesia occurred when a person's autobiographical memories became detached from his or her sense of personal identity. A problem with this idea is that it doesn't satisfactorily explain why some people experience this and others don't. The Freudian model of psychogenic amnesia (in particular, fugue) explains why patients are often found wandering and confused. Unconsciously, in a symbolic way, they are 'running away' from their anxiety.

RLA 22

1 Try this technique for yourself.

RLA 23

1 You must summarize using your own words.

2 It lacks ecological validity. Studies in the lab do not accurately mimic seeing an accident in real life (encoding) or recalling the information in a court room (retrieval).

3 Retrieval is an active process. People tend to generalize material when they retrieve it. People attempt to interpret new information within the context of their existing knowledge. Expectations influence the way in which material is retrieved (see 'Schema theory' on page 20 in Chapter 2).

R Selected references

Chapter 1

Bartlett, FC (1932). *Remembering*. Cambridge: Cambridge University Press.

Brown, R, and McNeill, D (1966). 'The "tip-of the tongue" phenomenon.' *Journal of verbal learning and verbal behaviour*, 5, pp. 325–37.

Buzan, T (1974). *Use your head*. BBC Publications.

Duncan, C (1949). 'The retroactive effect of electro-shock on learning.' *Journal of comparative physiology*, 42, pp. 32–44.

Gardner, R (1988). 'Psychiatric syndromes as infrastructure for intra-specific communication.' In MRA Chance (ed.) *Social fabrics of the mind*. Lawrence Earlbaum Associates, Hove and London; Hillsdale, NJ.

Haber, RN (1979). 'Twenty years of hunting eidetic imagery: Where's the ghost?' *The behavioural and brain sciences*, 2, pp. 583–629.

Hebb, DO (1949). *The organization of behaviour*. New York: Wiley.

Howell, P and Darwin, CJ (1977). 'Some properties of auditory memory for rapid format transitions.' *Memory and cognition*, 5, pp. 700–708.

James, W (1890). *Principles of psychology*. New York: Holt.

Kline, P (1972). *Fact and fantasy in Freudian theory*. London: Methuen.

Mandler, G (1980). 'Recognizing: the judgement of a previous occurrence.' *Psychological review*, 27, pp. 252–71.

Miller, GA (1956). 'The magical number seven, plus or minus two: some limits on our capacity for processing information.' *Psychological review*, 63, pp. 81–97.

Nunn, C (1996). *Awareness: What it is, what it does*. Routledge.

Parkin, AJ and Leng, NRC (1993). *Neuropsychology of amnesic syndromes*. Hove: Earlbaum.

Reber, AS (1985). *The Penguin dictionary of psychology*. Penguin Books Ltd.

Ryle, G (1949). *The concept of mind*. London: Hutchinson.

Scoville, WB and Milner, B (1957). 'Loss of recent memory after bilateral hippocampal lesions.' *Journal of neurology, neurosurgery and psychiatry*, 20, pp. 11–21.

Sperling, G (1960). 'The information available in brief visual presentations.' *Psychological monographs: general and applied*, 74, pp. 1–29.

Tinbergen, N (1951). *The study of instinct*. Oxford: Clarenden Press.

Tulving, E (1972). 'Episodic and semantic memory.' In E Tulving and W Donaldson (eds) *The organization of memory*, pp. 382–404. New York: Academic Press.

Chapter 2

Atkinson, RC and Shiffrin, RM (1968). 'Human memory: a proposed system and its control process.' In KW Spence and JT Spence (eds) *The psychology of learning and motivation* (vol. 2). London: Academic Press.

Baddeley, AD and Hitch, G (1974). 'Working memory.' In GH Bower (ed.) *Recent advances in learning and motivation* (vol. 8). New York: Academic Press.

Bartus, RT, Dean, RL, Beer, B and Lippa, AS (1982). 'The cholinergic hypothesis of geriatric memory dysfunction.' *Science*, 217, p. 408.

Bower, GH, Black, JB and Turner, TJ (1969). 'Scripts in memory for text.' *Cognitive psychology*, 11, pp. 177–220.

Chase, WG and Simon, HA (1973). 'Perception in chess.' *Cognitive psychology*, 4, pp. 55–81.

Collins, AM and Quillian, MR (1969). 'Retrieval time for semantic memory.' *Journal of verbal learning and verbal behaviour*, 8, pp. 240–47.

Conrad, R (1964). 'Acoustic confusion in immediate memory.' *British journal of psychology*, 55, pp. 75–84.

Craik, FIM and Lockhart, R (1972). 'Levels of processing.' *Journal of verbal learning and verbal behaviour*, 11, pp. 671–84.

Craik, FIM and Watkins, MJ (1973). 'The role of rehearsal in short term memory.' *Journal of verbal learning and verbal behaviour*, 12, pp. 599–607.

Eysenck, MW (1993). *Principles of cognitive psychology*. Hove: Earlbaum.

Glanzer, M and Cunitz, AR (1966). 'Two storage mechanisms in free recall.' *Journal of verbal learning and verbal behaviour*, 5, pp. 928–35.

Harris, JE and Sunderland, A (1981). 'A brief survey of the management of memory disorders in rehabilitation units in Britain.' *International rehabilitation medicine*, 3, pp. 206–209.

Intraub, H and Nicklos, S (1985). 'Levels of processing and picture memory: the physical superiority effect.' *Journal of experimental psychology: learning, memory and cognition*, 11, pp. 284–98.

Lloyd, P, Mayes, A, Manstead, ASR, Meudell, PR and Wagner, HL (1984). *Introduction to psychology: an integrated approach*. London: Fontana.

Murdock, BB (1962). 'The serial position effect in free recall.' *Journal of experimental psychology*, 64, pp. 482–88.

Paivio, A (1969). 'Mental imagery in association learning and memory.' *Psychological review*, 76, pp. 241–63.

Spilich, GJ, Vesonder, GT, Chiesi, HL and Voss, JF (1979). 'Text processing of domain-related information for individuals with high and low domain knowledge.' *Journal of verbal learning and verbal behaviour*, 18, pp. 275–90.

Wilding, J and Mohindra, N (1980). 'Effects of subvocal suppression, articulatory aloud and noise on sequence recall.' *British journal of psychology*, 71, pp. 247–61.

Woole, KA, Weber, A and Lowry, DH (1972). 'Bizarreness versus interaction of mental images as determinants of learning.' *Cognitive psychology*, 3, pp. 518–23.

Chapter 3

Abernathy, EM (1940). 'The effect of changed environmental conditions upon the results of college examinations.' *Journal of psychology*, 10, pp. 293–301.

Bahrick, HP, Bahrick, PO and Wittlinger, RP (1975). 'Fifty years of memory for names and faces: a cross sectional approach.' *Journal of experimental psychology: general*, 104, pp. 54–75.

Bower, GH and Hilgard, ER (1981). *Theories of learning*. Englewood Cliffs, NJ: Prentice Hall.

Brown, R and Kulik, J (1977). 'Flashbulb memories.' *Cognition*, 5, pp. 73–99.

Brunvand, H (1983). *The vanishing hitchhiker*. London: Picador.

Comfort, A (1976). *A good age*. New York: Simon and Schuster.

Engan, T and Ross, BM (1973). 'Long term memory of odors with and without verbal descriptions.' *Journal of experimental psychology*, 100, pp. 221–7.

Goodwin, DW, Powell, B, Bremer, B, Hoine, H and Stern, J (1969). 'Alcohol and recall: state dependent effects in man.' *Science*, 163, pp. 1358–60.

McGeoch, JA (1932). 'Forgetting and the law of disuse.' *Psychological review*, 39, pp. 352–70.

Mistry, J and Rogoff, B (1994). 'Remembering in cultural context.' In WJ Lonner and RS Malpass (eds) *Psychology and culture*. Boston: Alyn and Bacon.

Norman, DA (1981). 'Categorization of action slips.' *Psychological review*, 88, pp. 1–15.

Postman, L (1972). 'A pragmatic view of organization theory.' In E Tulving and W Donaldson (eds) *Organization of memory*. New York: Academic Press.

Reason, JT (1984). 'Absentmindedness and cognitive control.' In JE Harris and PE Morris (eds) *Everyday memory, actions and absentmindedness*. London: Academic Press.

Salthouse, TA (1991). 'Status of working memory as a mediator of adult age differences in cognition.' Address presented at APA, San Francisco, CA, August.

Sapolsky, RM (1998). *Why zebras don't get ulcers*. WH Freeman and Co.

Waldvogel, S (1948). 'The frequency and affective character of childhood memories.' *Psychological monographs*, 62, p. 291.

Wulf, F (1922). 'Uber die veranderung von vorstellungen.' *Psychologisch forschung*, 1, pp. 333–73.

Yesavage, JA (1983). 'Imagery retaining and memory training in the elderly.' *Gerontology*, 29, pp. 271–5.

Chapter 4

Berrington, WP, Liddell, DW and Foulds, GA (1956). 'A re-evaluation of the fugue.' *Journal of mental science*, 102, pp. 280–86.

Britt, SH (1975). 'Applying learning principles to

marketing.' *MSU business topics*, 23, pp. 5–12.

Bull, R and Rumsey, N (1988). *The social psychology of facial appearance*. New York: Springer-Verlag.

Claparede, E (1911). 'Recognition and moiite.' *Archives psycologiques Geneve*, 11, pp. 79–90.

Janet, P (1904). *Neuroses et idees fixes* (second edition). Paris: Felix Alcan.

Ley, P, Bradshaw, PW, Eaves, D and Walker, CM (1973). 'A method for increasing patients' recall of information presented by doctors.' *Psychological medicine*, 3, pp. 217–20.

Loftus, EF (1975). 'Leading questions and the eyewitness report.' *Cognitive psychology*, 1, pp. 560–72.

Luchins, AS (1959). 'Primacy-recency in impression formation.' In CI Hovland (ed.) *The order of presentation of persuasion*. New Haven, Conn: Yale University Press.

Lynch, JG and Srull, TK (1982). 'Memory and attentional factors in consumer choice: a review.' *Journal of consumer research*, 9, pp. 18–36.

McCloskey, M and Zaragoza, M (1985). 'Misleading information and memory for events: arguments and evidence against memory impairment hypothesis.' *Journal of experimental psychology: general*, 114, 3–18.

Squire, LR and Cohen, N (1982). 'Remote memory, retrograde amnesia and the neurophysiology of memory.' In LS Cermak (ed.) *Human memory and amnesia*, 275–305. Hillsdale, NJ: Earlbaum.

Taylor, S (1986). *Health psychology*. New York: Random House.

Weinstein, ND (1987). 'Unrealistic optimism about susceptibility to health problems: conclusions from a community wide sample.' *Journal of behavioural medicine*, 10, pp. 481–500.

Yarmey, AD (1983). 'Is the psychology of eyewitness identification a matter of common sense?' In Lloyd-Bostock, S and Clifford, B (eds) *Evaluating witness evidence*. Chichester: Wiley.

Index